General editor: Gra

Brodie's Notes on Jo

Heart of Darkness

Peter Washington MA MLitt

MACMILLAN

First published 1987 by Pan Books Ltd

Published 1992 by
MACMILLAN PRESS LTD
Houndmills, Basingstoke, Hampshire RG21 6XS
and London
Companies and representatives
throughout the world

ISBN 0–333–58068–0

10   9   8   7   6   5   4   3
03   02   01   00   99   98   97   96

Printed in Great Britain by
Mackays of Chatham PLC
Chatham, Kent

Contents

Page references in these Notes are to the
Penguin Classics edition of *Heart of Darkness*,
but as reference is also made to individual chapters,
the Notes may be used with any edition of the novella.

Preface

The intention throughout this study aid is to stimulate and guide, to encourage the reader's *involvement* in the text, to develop disciplined critical responses and a sure understanding of the main details.

Brodie's Notes provide a summary of the plot of the play or novel followed by act, scene or chapter summaries, each of which will have an accompanying critical commentary designed to emphasize the most important literary and factual details. Poems, stories or non-fiction texts will combine brief summary with critical commentary on either individual aspects or sequences of the genre being considered. Textual notes will be explanatory or critical (sometimes both), defining what is difficult or obscure on the one hand, or stressing points of character, style, plot or the technical aspects of poetry on the other. Revision questions will be set at appropriate points to test the student's careful application to the text of the prescribed book.

The second section of each of these study aids will consist of a critical examination of the author's art. This will cover such major elements as characterization, style, structure, setting, theme(s) for example in novels, plays or stories; in poetry it will deal with the types of poem, rhyme, rhythm, free verse for example, or in non-fiction with the main literary concerns of the work. The editor may choose to examine any aspect of the book being studied which he or she considers to be important. The paramount aim is to send the student back to the text. Each study aid will include a series of general questions which require detailed knowledge of the set book: the first of these questions will have notes by the editor of what *might* be included in a written answer. A short list of books considered useful as background reading for the student will be provided at the end.

The General Certificate of Secondary Education in Literature

These study aids are suitable for candidates taking the new GCSE examinations in English Literature since they provide detailed preparation for examinations in that subject as well as presenting critical ideas and commentary of major use to candidates preparing their coursework files. These aids provide a basic, individual and imaginative response to the appreciation of literature. They stimulate disciplined habits of reading, and they will assist the responsive student to analyse and to write about the texts with discrimination and insight.

Graham Handley

Literary terms used in these notes

novella Difficult to define except by negative, a novella is neither a short novel nor a long short story. It is a prose fiction which develops in full one aspect of a situation, whereas a novel develops several aspects and a short story deals with a fragment of experience. Were *Heart of Darkness* a novel, we would expect the other characters to play a far greater role in the action, and their relationships to be examined in more detail. A short story, on the other hand, would concentrate on one part of the episode – Marlow's meeting with Kurtz, for example; and there would be far less description.

irony Words are ironic when their meaning is the opposite of their literal sense. A situation is ironic when the person involved in it is unaware of its real significance; or when he realizes that significance and becomes conscious of the contradictions in it. Marlow, for example, takes part in the colonial adventure for his own profit, but understands the tragic implications of western exploitation in Africa.

image Literally meaning 'a visual representation', image has come to signify any figure of speech in which one thing is substituted for another, or compared with another.

symbol Something which stands for something else, usually a thing representing an idea or feeling.

Conrad: the man and his work

Given Conrad's status as a great English novelist, canonized by
F. R. Leavis in *The Great Tradition* (1948) a few years after his
death and intensively studied by other critics, it is still a matter
for curiosity that he was a Pole who always wished he had
decided to write in French. Typically, the great master of subtle
shades disliked the English language because of its large and
varied vocabulary which provides so many finely discriminated
varieties of meaning: to the end of his life Conrad took the view
that the lucidity of French would have been a more suitable
medium for the kind of novel he wished to write. In view of his
extraordinary success in the chosen tongue, we may put this
down to chronic melancholy and self-doubt; but there is no
doubt that he learnt at least as much – and probably more –
about the art of fiction from French writers than from the
English, whose tradition he so nobly carried on.

Conrad was born into a mildly aristocratic Polish family in
1857. Orphaned at an early age, he lived with his uncle in
Warsaw until he took the decisive step of moving to Marseilles at
the age of sixteen in order to become a sailor. This was not a
typical ambition for the Polish aristocracy, who habitually went
into the army if they wished to join a service, and it marks
Conrad out from the start as a solitary and something of a misfit.
In 1877, overwhelmed by debts and frustrated in his naval
career, Conrad attempted suicide: the bullet providentially went
straight through his chest, just missing the heart, and so began
the development of a great English novelist; for Conrad, dis-
gusted with France, decided to try his luck in England, where he
eventually succeeded in becoming Master in the Merchant Navy,
incidentally learning the necessary English language on the way.
In 1886 he became a British subject, and in 1889, while holi-
daying in London began his first novel, *Almayer's Folly*, published
in 1895, when Conrad was 38. The thirty years of English fiction
which followed thus owe a good deal to the French Merchant
Marine and a young man's unsteady hand.

Conrad's writing life was relatively short, when compared with
the spans of his contemporaries: Wells, Shaw, Galsworthy, Wal-
pole and Bennett; but he is far and away the most difficult and
the most distinguished novelist of his generation, and this may

have something to do with his alien status in England where, though he married and had children, he was never entirely at home. One thing characterising contemporary English writers, notably lacking in Conrad, is *cosiness*, the easy sense of familiarity with readers, the feeling that writer and audience understand one another almost too well. For all his narrative gift – his ability to grip the attention and hold it – there is nothing easy or comfortable about Conrad: he is constantly aware of the strange, the awkward, the disturbing elements in his stories and this puts him in a fascinating relationship with the English tradition of which he is now held to be a part. The dominant tone of the novel in late nineteenth-century England – which can be felt in all the writers named above – was established by Dickens (1812–70) who, despite his early death, continued to exercise a powerful influence for many decades afterwards. Dickens's presentation of English life is far more extraordinary than we often think: he had a profound influence on Dostoyevsky (1821–81) and later on Kafka (1883–1924), whose terrifying explorations in the spiritual underworld are unimaginable without his example; but he was also a powerful force in establishing that cosy, Christmassy, clean-cut, virtuous image of the Englishman which was to be such a feature of literature – and more especially, popular literature – in the century following. What is so fascinating about Conrad is that – especially in *Heart of Darkness* and *Lord Jim* – he brings together the two forces which in Dickens's work are kept separate: the heroic Englishman and the sinister forces lurking in Man's spiritual depths. Thus in one incarnation, Marlow might be a figure out of Henty (1832–1902) or Haggard (1856–1925), immensely popular writers of adventure stories in Conrad's own time; but in another, he resembles more a Dostoyevskyan or Kaftaesque protagonist, spiritually tortured, involved in grotesque adventures with a cast of fantastic figures, in exotic surroundings.

It is clear from Conrad's various writings that he both admired what he saw as the distinctive character of the English, yet felt remote from it. And, admiring the extraordinary gifts and determination which had created an empire and also a remarkably high standard of personal conduct among its cultivated classes, he was also aware of the fragile basis such achievements rested on. Besides this, Conrad was himself a profoundly melancholic man who believed in work, in the practical tasks of everyday life, as the only possible palliative for such melancholy – just as Marlow does – and he was therefore well aware of both the power of the avowed English commitment to practical life – for which the nation was famous – and its dangers; chief of which is to pretend that emotional and spiritual problems simply do not exist. By the end of the nineteenth century England had become a kind of model for all European nations, who envied her power and success – and also resented it; and the Belgians, in *Heart of Darkness*, are, to some extent, aping the English. What they lack is what Conrad admired in the English empire proper: an extreme, almost suicidal sense of selflessness, service and duty. These are the qualities which – if any can – justify the imperial adventure; and, in the absence of a metaphysically grounded ethical system, now that men no longer believe in God, offer the only possibility of a more general and developed morality. It was these qualities which the novelist learnt to respect during his years at sea.

As this description suggests, Conrad was both a realist and a romantic. Awareness of human vulnerability and the severe limitations on achievement of any kind made him at once pessimistic about human behaviour and full of admiration. In Conrad's eyes, to survive at all is a major achievement; and to develop beyond that a life which is more than self-preservation is a constantly repeated miracle at which we can only wonder. All too often, even self-preservation eludes us, and if one claims that Conrad's outlook was fundamentally tragic, that is why. His three great novels – *Nostromo* (1904) *The Secret Agent* (1907), and *Under Western Eyes* (1911) –are all stories of failure. Interestingly enough, they are also stories which touch largely on politics; and although *Heart of Darkness* makes little obvious allusion to political life, it is a submerged theme in that story, too. Politics is the arena in which the organization – and therefore the morality – of social life is debated and decided; and although Conrad, in the nineteenth-century tradition, habitually concentrates on a small number of characters, he is deeply interested in the social context of their actions, and the larger meaning of those actions. In *Nostromo*, the personal fate of Charles Gould, owner of the silver mine, is inextricably involved with the fate of his country, the republic of Costaguana. In *The Secret Agent*, Mr and Mrs Verloc, and her half-witted brother, Stevie, are destroyed by Verloc's involvement with anarchism. Anarchism is also the theme of *Under Western Eyes*; and it plays a part in other shorter works by Conrad. Given the persistent association of this novelist with sea-stories – which he himself resented – this is a most important point. In *Heart of Darkness*, the political background is crucial. If it were not for the activities of European colonists in Africa, the story would not arise. Furthermore, the activity is a very specific one – not merely political colonization, but economic exploitation. The personal fates of Marlow and Kurtz are dependent on this fact: ivory is to them what silver is to Gould – a precious commodity which turns out to be a destructive force, just as violent as the bomb which kills Stevie in *The Secret Agent*. Political violence was unfamiliar to the great English middle-class reading public: there had been no revolution in England since the seventeenth century, and no war on English soil for some hundreds of years. All Conrad's great fiction was written before the cataclysm of 1914, but he had personal experience of violence as a child in a Poland dominated by the Russians: the novelist was orphaned as a direct consequence of the privations endured by his parents in Russian exile, as a punishment for their revolutionary activities. For him, as for all Central Europeans, politics unavoidably meant violence and repression.

Conrad found writing just as difficult a process as living. Suffering from periods of profound melancholia and self-doubt, and struggling for almost five years in an alien language with his first novel, he never wrote with fluency, though his output is substantial. Sometimes he collaborated on work, and several stories were written with his fellow novelist Ford Madox Ford (1873–1939), whose *The Good Soldier* (1915) is one of the period's classic texts. Despite these difficulties – and perhaps, in part, this was their cause – Conrad always continued to experiment. Among recent writers his two great masters were Flaubert (1821–80) and Henry James (1843–1916), who was himself a disciple of Flaubert. Both these writers preached the gospel of technical perfection. They took the view that writing was not a natural activity, in which one poured out the soul, but a highly demanding craft, in which the writer's primary object was to find just the right words for what he or she had to say. They were also committed to a theory of form which held that writing is not simply a mirror of reality – though it does portray what we know in the world – but has its own laws, which must be observed. What matters about a novel for Flaubert and James are its aesthetic qualities: it is, above all, a work of art, not a social record or the pastime of an idle hour. Both writers had a lofty view of art as that activity which is most characteristically human; and both created a series of masterpieces in which technical problems of extreme difficulty are triumphantly surmounted. Among these technical problems, one which – quite

naturally – preoccupied them was the problem of narration.
How is the story to be told? From what point or points of view?
In what tone? To what purpose?

These were questions which also interested Conrad, and we
can see him mulling them over even in a short work such as
Heart of Darkness. Consider how the story is told. The principal
narrator is, apparently, Conrad himself, who forms one of the
audience aboard the *Nellie*. But once Marlow starts to speak,
Conrad recedes almost completely into the background: only
very occasionally, before the end, is Marlow's narrative flow
broken by the author's interjections. But within Marlow's tale
there are other narrators who tell him about Kurtz before he
ever reaches the man – and even within *their* tales there are other
narrators still: Conrad, for example, tells us what Marlow says
the Patched Man had said about what Kurtz told *him*. And from
the Chief Brickmaker we learn what the Company in Europe
thinks about Marlow and Kurtz. The novella is like a series of
Chinese boxes, one within the other. And that is not all; for
within the various narratives Conrad also experiments with time
and sequence; in a striking passage on p.84 (Penguin Classics
edition), for example, Marlow's confused excitement impels him
to anticipate later elements of his story, to mix his meeting with
the Intended, with his meetings with Kurtz – whom, at this
stage, he hasn't even met once. Such a telescoping of the narrative perspective gives a vivid insight into the impact Kurtz has
made on Marlow, and it also tells us how difficult Marlow is
finding it to make sense of his experience, which rushes upon
him disrupting the even flow of the story, just as Kurtz has
disrupted the even flow of Marlow's life. In *Heart of Darkness*
such experimental techniques are particularly appropriate, for a
major theme of the novella is the extreme difficulty of narrating
the kind of encounter Marlow has had; but the problem of
making some sense out of the baffling world is a persistent
concern of Conrad's in all his work. Narrative is a way of establishing order: one thing happens, then another happens, after
it, or even because of it. A causal chain is described, helping us to
understand the meaning of events. Conrad, often doubtful
about whether events *did* have any meaning, yet constrained, if
he was to write novels at all, to arrange things in patterns,
derives much of his power as a story-teller from the conflict
between these two domains: the chaos of experience and the
order of art. At his best, he walks a fine line between them.

Plot

It might well be said that *Heart of Darkness* has no plot – or, at least that such plot as it does have is irrelevant: what matters is not the causal sequence of events, not even the emotional significance they have for the two main characters – Kurtz and Marlow – but the extraordinary verbal texture of the story, its dense network of metaphors and allusions. If we ask ourselves What happens? in the simple physical sense, we can reply: Marlow journeys up the Congo, where he meets a dying agent whose letters he takes back to the agent's fiancée in Brussels. That would tell us almost nothing about a story which depends entirely upon how it is narrated. Yet it would be equally unfair to insist that what happens in the story is of no importance at all. Unlike almost all his contemporary novelists, Conrad had been a man of action himself, and his stories are invariably concerned with the active life: Marlow constantly reminds us that this is what he clings to in order to avoid excessive introspection. So we must concede that if the plot – who did what to whom – is of little importance, what happens matters a great deal. One might say that *activity* counts for more than *action*. The high profile of a developed plot is replaced by the seamless texture of deeds, occurrences, opinions and feelings, woven together in a tight linguistic tapestry. This is not so much Marlow's adventure, as an idea's – the idea of darkness: literal and metaphorical, physical, emotional and psychological. What we want instead of plot analysis is an account of what happens to this idea: the meeting between Kurtz and Marlow, which forms the anti-climactic climax of the novella, is no more than a peg to hang it on.

As if to emphasize this point, the novella is distinguished not by the development of relationships among the characters, but by the lack of such development. Plot depends upon interaction: X's behaviour impinges on B, the circumstances in place Z determine the behaviour of person Y. Nothing of the kind can be found in *Heart of Darkness*. The central character, the narrator Marlow, conspicuously fails to relate positively to any of the other characters – or, at least, they fail to relate to him. The aunt, the manager, Kurtz, Kurtz's Intended, the patched man, all get it wrong: Marlow persistently finds himself at cross-purposes with them; and the narrative constantly alerts us to what is *not* happening, *not* being communicated or understood. In the same negative sense the text's people resist relationship with their surroundings: Brussels is not a living city but a whited sepulchre; the stations are hopelessly at odds with the continent they purport to control; the two drawing rooms Marlow visits in Europe convey a strong air of unreality; even the boat, where he feels most at home, shows signs of alienation, working against its captain rather than for him. Throughout the story, places and people, people and people, do not engage. At the end, returning to Europe, Marlow feels even more out of things than he did in the frightening jungle: his encounter with darkness has made everything seem unreal. The one exception to this lack of engagement is, of course, the darkness itself, as embodied in Africa: that dark continent which affects those who venture into it beyond all expectation – unless, like the Chief Accountant and the Manager, they cling fiercely and negatively to a parody of 'civilized' behaviour. Yet even Africa does not play the common role of locales in late nineteenth-century fiction, which dwells almost obsessively upon the determining details of specific environments and the part they play in shaping the lives of the characters. Ibsen's middle-class Norway, Hardy's proletarian Dorset, the Paris of Zola and Proust, the provincial France of Conrad's great master, Flaubert – are all in their ways exact; so, for that matter, is the fictional South American republic of Conrad's supreme masterpiece *Nostromo*, or the London of his wonderful *The Secret Agent*. But the Africa of *Heart of Darkness* remains studiously vague and generalized: that, indeed, is a major source of its power, both in the book and, Conrad implies, in fact. The only character in the text who has engaged fully with it – Kurtz – has gone more or less mad. There are many other examples in fiction of a place obsessing or even maddening a character – the almost contemporary Christminster of Hardy's *Jude the Obscure* (1896) springs to mind – but in every case it is the attributes of that place which do the work. Conrad's Africa is distinguished by its very lack of attributes, its formlessness; such qualities as it has are described in negative terms – it is an abyss, an emptiness, a darkness, an immense, unfathomable profundity. Thus we are faced with a paradox: beyond destroying the health of just about every white man who ventures there, Africa exerts no specific influence on the characters or the plot; on the other hand, it is absolutely pervasive in the book, from the pre-echo of its darkness on the very first page. This paradox is resolved only if we think of the persistently negative ways

Conrad uses to describe it: for the continent exerts its decisive influence on everything in the text by very virtue of its mystery, its absences, its hidden, unknown nature. And this, in turn, is why the *action* of the book is of such comparatively minor importance: for the effect of what is absent or negative can only be well described through consciousness of such absence or negativity. It is this point which gives us the clue to Conrad's topic: not *action* – or even the *activity* Marlow desperately devises to mask the lack of action – but the uneasy, disturbing consciousness of things normally ignored, which the mysterious African silence and stillness – 'immobility' is a favourite word in this book – constantly evoke. For what is revealed by Marlow's encounter with Africa is not – as many commentators have thought – a discovery of the self; but, on the contrary, the terrifying sense that there may not be such a self; that underneath the civilized surface there is only the formless chaos of the forest. Readers have seen in this story a version of the quest theme – the search for some hidden object, which shapes the plot. If that is so, the search concludes with the discovery of a further mystery, and the plot is left unresolved.

Chapter summaries, critical commentaries, textual notes and revision questions

Chapter 1

As twilight falls, five companions gather aboard the *Nellie*, moored in the Thames. One of them, Marlow, tells the story of his voyage up the Congo. The adventure began, he says, when his aunt got him a job as captain of a river steamer, with the company which controlled the Congo territory. After a brief interview and medical inspection in Brussels, he says goodbye to his aunt and leaves for Africa, aboard a French ship. The voyage takes four weeks. At the mouth of the river he transfers to a steamer for the two hundred mile journey up river, to meet his own boat. Arriving at the Company Station, he meets the Chief Accountant, who refers to the mysterious Mr Kurtz. After ten days there, Marlow has to trek a further two hundred miles through the forest to the Central Station, a trip which takes fifteen days, partly because Marlow is hampered by his ineffectual white companion. He arrives to find his steamer wrecked and the manager furious, because they are late. At the Central Station, Marlow also meets his passengers – other company agents – and the 'Chief Brickmaker', who pumps him for information about his European connections. They discuss the mysterious Kurtz. The Eldorado Exploring Expedition arrives, led by the manager's uncle, but without the expected rivets needed to mend the steamer.

Commentary

The chapter begins by establishing the setting in which the story is told – a crucial move, given Conrad's desire to direct our attention to the comparison between Europe and Africa, between the city and the wilderness. The Thames and the Congo both wind into the heart of an area, not only literally but symbolically: they stand for everything we associate with their locations. These locations are very different: England is a great commercial empire, the most advanced society in the world at the time in which Conrad writes; while Central Africa is perhaps the most remote and primitive. So, at least, it seems; but Conrad makes a link between the two through the symbolism of the river and through the colouring – dark, sombre, mysterious – he gives to both; and by invoking the distant past, he also suggests that perhaps the differences between Europe and Africa, England and the Congo, are more apparent than real. The other crucial thing to be established in the opening pages is the character of Marlow. This is done in two ways: in his own words, and by showing his relationship to his audience, especially to the anonymous narrator, Conrad himself. Marlow's consciousness is the link between the two points of reference – London and the Inner Station – which both reflect on him and are illuminated by his discourse. As the story develops we find it increasingly difficult to disentangle Marlow's growing awareness – and his growing perplexity – from the intricate development of the theme stated at the outset, the theme of his 'culminating experience'.

The complicated relationship between settings and persons is a feature of the novella throughout. When Marlow reaches Brussels, for example, he finds an analogy between the appearance of a town which always 'makes me think of a white sepulchre' (35) and the behaviour of the people in it. The same is true when he later reaches the Congo, and again when he returns to Brussels to meet the Intended in her drawing-room. The first chapter as a whole covers Marlow's introduction to the 'theme' of the Congo and the associated 'theme' of Kurtz. At this stage of the book, Marlow is still primarily preoccupied with organizing his trip up the river as a job – which means getting his boat repaired. His obsession with Kurtz has not yet developed. In consequence, this is the most straightforward chapter of the three, filled with comic touches, and only faintly coloured by the ominous shades of what is to come, and about which we have been warned at the book's beginning. Marlow has a series of encounters – tinged with a sardonic comedy we would now be inclined to call black – with his aunt, the officials in the Company office, the Chief Accountant, the Manager and the Brickmaker. Each one is carefully used to build up the story and to introduce preparatory material about Kurtz. Particularly important are the conflicting impressions we receive. Marlow's aunt takes an absurdly idealistic view of colonial activities, echoed at the book's end by Kurtz's Intended. The Company clerk has a rather different attitude, and the employees on the spot all show different aspects of the imperial adventure: unimaginative and self-seeking (the Manager), detached (the Chief Accountant), ambitious and cynical (the Brickmaker). It is no wonder that

Marlow begins to feel sympathy for Kurtz in the light of their behaviour.

yawl Small sailing boat or yacht. The syntax of the opening paragraph is somewhat unclear. Does 'it' refer to the boat or to its occupants? Presumably it is they – and not the wind – who are 'bound down the river', and waiting for the tide to turn so they can begin their voyage. This slight uncertainty, however, is not untypical of Conrad: it is not always possible to tell when he intends it and when confusion arises from the subtle complexity of his prose. For this reason, the reader of *Heart of Darkness* needs to be constantly alert.

sea-reach Stretch of water leading to the sea.

offing Stretch of water visible from the boat.

interminable . . . Already, in the sixth line of the story, Conrad introduces the note of mystery and infinity, taken up over and again in these first pages.

sprits Diagonal rods intended to extend fore-and-aft sails. Conrad's training and career aboard sailing-ships gives him an easy mastery of all the terminology and a slightly romantic affection for them which the later lines on English naval history (29) reveal. The *Nellie* is sharply contrasted in its clean elegance with the ropy steamer Marlow sails up the Congo.

air was dark Already the story's key word appears in para 1. It is darkness on the river which brings the story to Marlow's mind, by association; but, as his opening reflections reveal, he is also well aware of the profounder connections between the 'dark' continent, the remote past of European civilizations and the darkness of human hearts.

motionless Immobility and silence are constantly evoked by Marlow to characterize the banks of the Congo. Here they are prefigured. The 'greatest town' is not so far from the African heart of darkness.

pilot The image of the pilot is to prove significant through the story. Marlow pilots the steamer through the dangerous waters of the Congo, but he also pilots his readers into the heart of the mystery. Kurtz, by contrast, who has set himself up as a pilot (guide) to the natives, fails them.

luminous . . . gloom Notice the contrast between the river and the bank. For the sailor the river, however unpredictable or dangerous, is friendlier, less of a mystery, than the bank. Water is luminous, it moves, it lives, it gives life: these symbolic associations are also present to us when we read. Even the frightening Congo is less disturbing than the vast landmass which encloses it.

the bond of the sea . . . A phrase which resonates throughout Conrad's work, signifying a number of things: male comradeship, danger faced and shared, a romantic sense of the compulsion always to return to the sea, a complex symbol for existence itself, as a boat afloat in a mysterious and probably hostile universe.

Lawyer . . . Notice Conrad's constant resort to type-names: Aunt, The Intended etc. This does two things: it gives the story an almost mythical feeling, designating the characters as types; and it makes Marlow and Kurtz stand out from the rest.

somewhere Marlow is the narrator of several other stories by Conrad: *Lord Jim* (1900), *Chance* (1913) and 'Youth' (1902). Observe how quietly Conrad inserts himself into the narrative. Within seven pages he has effectively retired from it, with only one or two important later interpolations.

bones Dominoes.

aft In the stern of the vessel.

mizzen-mast The mast nearest the stern.

idol This is a curious pre-echo of Kurtz, who becomes a kind of god to the natives.

pacifically . . . Notice how Conrad brilliantly moves this passage of description from luminous calm to troubled darkness, as though to anticipate the progress of Marlow's story; and notice, too, how the gloom comes out of the west – not from Africa, the south.

The old river . . . Conrad here introduces an important historical perspective. At first it seems that the river is bringing to Marlow's mind the heroic deeds of the past: Raleigh and Drake sailing out to thrash the Spaniards etc. But a closer reading reveals that there is a deeper, more complicated theme: the pursuit of wealth and glory which leads to the development of empires and commonwealths. That is a positive way of putting it; looked at negatively this pursuit is also the origin of colonialism and exploitation. The crucial point here is that the same phenomena can be seen to have two sides not easily separable – good and bad, glorious and vile. The ambiguity foreshadows Kurtz's career. He, too, was seemingly a bearer of the 'sacred fire' whose mission ended in horror. He, too, is in a sense 'great' – but the ambiguity forces us to ask ourselves what this means. The problem is that without the sort of men who have the energy and vision for such enterprises, humanity would never progress at all – yet does such a high price have to be paid for progress as to render it futile? And there is a deeper mystery still underlying this moral dilemma, for Conrad's insistence on river images, especially on the inevitable ebb and flow of the river, subtly hints that such human developments are not simply a matter of human choice: we do not elect to progress or remain static, to colonize or to be colonized. Stronger forces are at work within us: the forces of nature which make the tropical forest also help to form our motives and desires, and it is desires which drive us on, rather than rational choices. If the result – a town, an empire – *looks* rational, contact with the primitive will soon show it to be something otherwise. This is one of the lessons Marlow learns on the Congo. Here, the memories of glory are shown to be a decisive force in urging on the English to their empire.

Sir Francis Drake 1543–96. The greatest of the Elizabethan adventurers.

Sir John Franklin Victorian explorer, lost in the Arctic.
Golden Hind Drake's flagship.
Erebus and *Terror* Two ships in Franklin's expedition.
'Change The Stock Exchange.
sacred fire This phrase, which seems to refer to the notion of
  something divine in Man, urging him on, becomes ironic in the
  context of the story's development. Kurtz's motivation brings the
  nature of the 'sacred fire' into question.
fairway Navigable channel.
gloom in sunshine This paradox reflects the paradox of the story, the
  perplexing relationship between good and evil.
And this . . . Marlow's first words underline the story's symbolism, and
  the Europe/Africa link.
most seamen . . . Here Conrad emphasizes the point I made earlier:
  for sailors, water is more secure than land.
a whole continent . . . This sentence reflects ironically on what is to
  come, anticipating Marlow's own explanation of how he deliberately
  clings to superficial realities to save himself from excessive
  introspection. But Marlow is here also distinguished from ordinary
  seamen in his approach to stories. The character described is really
  part of Conrad himself.
trireme A kind of galley with three sets of rowers.
the Gauls The inhabitants of part of what is now France.
legionaries Roman soldiers.
end of the world . . . The comparison is appropriate. To the ancient
  world Britain was the end of the earth, the most distant point
  westwards to which anyone had ever travelled. To the Roman
  historian Tacitus (c.AD55–120) the Britons represented the barbarism
  nineteenth-century Europeans saw in Africa.
Falernian A district in Campania, Central Italy, famous in antiquity for
  its wine.
dying like flies The phrase anticipates the scene which greets Marlow
  in Africa.
Ravenna The town – once a port – in Northern Italy where the
  Adriatic fleet was based.
toga The garment worn by adult male citizens of the Roman empire. It
  denoted privilege.
incomprehensible Marlow approaches his topic sideways, through the
  Romans. The 'fascination' is something he will return to.
Buddha The founder of Buddhism (sixth century BC) who is
  characteristically portrayed in a meditative position, like the idol
  referred to on p.28.
efficiency . . . a squeeze Here Marlow elaborates a central theme: the
  relationship of colonialism – with its avowed civilizing mission – to
  mere exploitation. Efficiency saves in two senses: it prevents the
  colonizers from degenerating into mere looters, and it gives a purpose
  to their conquest. As Marlow says later in the same paragraph, it is the
  idea that matters, not the reality of colonization – though he gives a

strong hint that this is a consolation only to the colonizers, not to their subjects. We must also remember that Marlow's view is not necessarily either the narrator's, or Conrad's. As it happens, Conrad felt about empires what Forster said about armies: he admired soldiers but he hated war.

inconclusive This remark alerts the reader to the nature of Marlow's story, and reminds us that it *is* a story i.e., a tale told to an audience who are part of the larger narrative framework.

personally The effect of his experience on Marlow is, of course, the core of the story: what happens is crucially mediated through his understanding of it.

a heavenly mission Marlow's remarks ironically anticipate the story he is going to tell. It is, after all, the settled, married men who best represent civilization. Marlow is a kind of wandering savage.

a passion for maps... This passage is autobiographical. As a boy, Conrad did what Marlow does – and his finger landed on the Congo.

not so nasty... In this humorous dig at English xenophobia – suspicion of 'abroad' – Conrad makes a serious point about the strangeness of foreigners: the Africans are the strangest foreigners of all so far as Europeans are concerned, but equally the European 'civilized' nations dislike one another.

a glorious idea The aunt's letter picks up Marlow's word (p.32). Conrad's satirical treatment of the aunt makes one wonder if Marlow is speaking ironically. This suspicion is confirmed a few lines later, on p.34, when Marlow refers to the 'noble cause', which he obviously sees as anything but.

A calamity The calamity is European occupation. With deepening irony Marlow speaks of 'the cause of progress' and 'this glorious affair'.

whited sepulchre A Biblical term meaning hypocrite: something fair without and foul within.

A narrow... Notice the careful description of the Company Office and the surgery; and the general evocation of Brussels. The city's apparent emptiness prepares us for the jungle's.

a shining map... The colours indicate colonial occupation. Red is British, blue French, purple German and yellow Belgian.

fascinating – deadly The combination exactly foreshadows the effect of Africa on men like Kurtz.

pale plumpness This Dickensian characterization of the Company Head gives us, through its absurdity, a sense of how *in*glorious the whole operation is. The next sentence, with its contrast between the man's short stature and the vast wealth he controls, takes up the point comically.

desolation and sympathy A rendering of what the secretary probably said in French – a more rhetorical language than English. Marlow is still being ironic – making the point that one man, more or less, is nothing to this great concern.

not quite right Marlow hardly needs to make this point: his irony has already told us as much. This is an example – there are quite a few – of Conrad overdoing things.

Ave! ... Morituri te salutant Hail ... those who are about to die salute you. These were the words with which gladiators in the arena addressed the Roman emperor.

a young chap Notice Conrad's brilliantly economical characterizing and using of this figure. In one paragraph he tells us everything he said in the previous, inferior, one.

Plato The Greek philosopher. The crude joke exactly hits off the clerk's callous vulgarity.

measure my head Anthropometry or head-measuring was all the rage among nineteenth-century anthropologists. It was thought to be a way of distinguishing between races, or even of estimating character.

alienist Specialist in mental diseases.

Englishman ... The point about this passage is that Englishmen were thought to be characteristically taciturn in the nineteenth century. Marlow harps on his Englishness here and there – especially in the slang he uses – but he *is* unlike the stereotype in his loquacity and talent for storytelling.

exceptional ... This exaggeration is of a piece with Kurtz's reputation, but in conflict with the view, held by the doctor and clerk, that no one of any importance would go out to the Congo if they could help it. On the one hand the aunt's remoteness from reality is emphasized; on the other, the company's hypocrisy.

such rot ... *Heart of Darkness* was written in the hey-day of European imperial propaganda, when nations were simultaneously scrambling for what colonial possessions they could get, while masking their economic and military self-interest with grand rhetoric about the White Man's Burden, the Christian Mission etc. It should be said that many people besides Marlow's aunt – serious people, deeply involved in the administration of colonial empires – sincerely believed in some of this rhetoric, especially in Britain, which had by far the largest, oldest and most substantial empire. Others, like Marlow himself, talked more realistically about profit.

blamed Damned.

enigma The idea of mystery, secrecy, the hidden, is central to the story – as is the discovery that what is hidden is no glorious truth but a squalid reality.

natural In one sense this word is opposed to 'civilized'.

nothing happened This episode anticipates the fusillade of the pilgrims (p.81) and emphasizes the futility of the European engagement with Africa: 'firing into a continent' is a telling phrase.

enemies ... The natives are persistently referred to as enemies, rebels, criminals etc. as Marlow later notices.

Nature Compare the personification of Nature here with the use of 'natural' on the previous page (p.40). We are aware throughout the story of a force – call it Nature – which works both through men and against them. It seems just as 'natural' to kill, steal and exploit – like the Europeans – as to submit and wonder, like the natives. This suggests that the opposition of 'natural' and 'civilized' noted above is transcended by the higher order of Nature in which everything is 'natural', whether good or bad.

mangroves Trees growing especially in swamps.

wallowing The confusion of organic and mechanical things is vital here. In this climate, everything rots, and even machines take on the quality of plants or animals, just as the wretched natives are made into machines.

reclaimed Marlow develops the ironic theme of progress.

so much alike This is a grimly humorous reversal of the usual European claim that black/brown/yellow men are indistinguishable.

the devil The book is suffused with hell imagery: devils, fiends, fire, torture, darkness etc.

flabby These words echo the description of the company head on p.36.

mournful stillness The contrast between the physical stillness of the forest with the noises emerging out of it is a constant motif.

work Marlow's exclamation echoes ironically his aunt's talk about 'workers'.

bundles ... angles A phrase which brilliantly evokes the transformation of the natives into *things* by the Belgian colonists.

He was ... ear A sentence which epitomizes the ironic treatment meted out to the Europeans by Marlow, and echoing his judgement on the company head. The sentence is superbly anti-climatic.

a distaste for the work This quiet sentence sums up all the evil of colonialism in one phrase.

Mr Kurtz The first we hear of him.

caravan Group of travellers with native bearers.

lamentable A curious combination of two senses: 'lamenting' and 'unfortunate'.

opening into a darkness ... The sense that the Manager is 'hollow' anticipates the hollowness of Kurtz and his claims – but it also anticipates Marlow's nihilistic suspicion that, at the heart of mystery, there is nothing – and that it is this discovery which has ruined Kurtz. The manager is able to avoid making such a discovery: he seals off his own interior from himself.

facts of life Compare Marlow and the Manager. Both cling to the surface of things, but Marlow is forced by character and circumstance to look below.

pilgrims Marlow's ironic name for the Company agents. There is nothing religious about their mission.

a small sketch ... We hear no more about this picture, and it is passed over quickly, but the symbolic significance is both ambiguous and ironic. Though the figure carries a torch – standing for illumination – it is blindfolded, and the torch makes little impact on the background. Even more tellingly, the figure is a woman – and in this story European women epitomize self-delusion and false idealism. We later discover that Kurtz's Intended is dignified and stately, like the woman in the painting, and we make the connection. Compare this picture with the description of her in the drawing-room at the end of the book.

We want... The 'brickmaker' is contemptuous and resentful. He speaks as though quoting from official correspondence.

gang of virtue The two words contradict one another, expressing both what the brickmaker thinks and what Marlow also believes: that such people are no better, and perhaps worse, being hypocrites.

Heap of muffs Gang of fools.

papier-mâché Pulped paper. The image expresses both the demoniac quality and the hollowness of the brickmaker.

pitch dark Appropriately, the story is told in darkness. Marlow's disembodied voice adds to the dreamlike quality, which he has himself emphasized.

from dictation i.e. he does what the manager tells him.

Your own reality... Compare Marlow's comment (p.57) 'We live, as we dream – alone.' Solitude is a major theme in this book and in Conrad's work generally: it entails the radical uncertainty of all knowledge – trapped in ourselves, we can never be certain about anything outside – or, indeed, within, given that we have nothing to measure our experience by absolutely, except its own satisfaction or frustration. It is solitude which also makes moral judgements so difficult: if we do not really understand the motivation and behaviour of others, what claim have we to pronounce on it? This point becomes important when Marlow is trying to work out his attitude to Kurtz, later in the book.

a good worker But this is real work – not the aunt's kind. Conrad has the practical man's profound respect for those who *do* something, however small, in the world.

ichthyosaurus Prehistoric reptile.

Eldorado The golden land imagined by the Spanish conquerors of America – therefore any place where money can be made easily.

moral ideas Here the phrase is used without irony.

Revision questions on Chapter 1

1 Why are the five introductory pages so important?

2 How does Conrad characterize Marlow, and by what means does he establish this character?

3 What contribution to the development of the story is made by the minor characters in this chapter?

4 In what ways does Conrad use the imagery of light and dark, and to what end?

5 Can we learn anything about the colonial relationship between Europe and Africa from this chapter?

Chapter 2

Lying concealed on his boat, Marlow overhears a conversation between the manager and his uncle on the bank: their topic is the difficulty of getting rid of Kurtz, who stands between the manager and promotion. Finally, Marlow and the Chief Engineer succeed in mending the boat, and the expedition sets off, including the manager and the other company agents. The Eldorado Explorers meanwhile vanish into the jungle for ever. Fifty miles short of Kurtz's station (the Inner Station) Marlow finds a stack of recently chopped wood on the bank, beside a dilapidated cottage, containing a mystifyingly annotated naval manual. There is also a cryptic warning message. Setting sail again, they are delayed by snags in the gradually narrowing river, and a thick fog, which comes and goes with great rapidity. Out of this fog emerge terrifying wailing noises, and when it lifts and the boat continues, a spear and arrow attack is mounted from the bank. The helmsman is killed and the 'pilgrims' fire back with their guns, but the attackers are only dispersed by the boat's steam-whistle. After tipping the helmsman overboard, and resolving to retreat, Marlow continues a little way up the river and suddenly comes upon the Inner Station, where they are greeted by a young man in patches, who turns out to be the former inhabitant of the dilapidated hut.

Commentary

The main topic of this chapter is the journey up the Congo. With the boat repaired, Marlow and his passengers set off, leaving behind the comparatively recognizable environment of the settlements, plunging into an alien landscape. At the same time, Marlow traces his own increasing introversion: the journey inland is paralleled by a journey within; the more remote the expedition becomes from familiar things, the more Marlow begins to discover in himself unfamiliar experiences. The presence of the invisible Kurtz looms larger and larger, as they get nearer to him, and Marlow begins to discover more about him. But notice also how much of the material about Kurtz in this chapter must have been discovered by Marlow later, when he meets the Patched Man. The obvious point of bringing it in here is to associate Marlow's journey into himself with his discovery of Kurtz. Retrospectively, the two are identified in his mind: the trip up river is a trip towards Kurtz. As if to emphasize this point, the chapter opens with Marlow overhearing a conversation about the agent, and ends with him meeting the Patched Man, who is to be his chief source of information.

In between these two moments, Conrad develops the elements of a conventional adventure story – native attacks, hidden dangers, the finding of abandoned huts – in a most unconventional way, by loading each event with symbolic significance. In fact, relatively little happens, if we compare this story with a full-blown adventure tale, but the atmosphere is so powerful, that we are gripped by what does *not* occur: our attention is constantly directed to silence, stillness, emptiness, immobility. We also become aware of the tensions on the boat between Marlow and his passengers; of their own rivalries, the incipient jealousy of Kurtz and – most important of all – the internal drama which is developing within Marlow himself.

Make rain and fine weather A literal translation from the French, meaning someone with great power or influence.

Invoice The implication here is that Kurtz has accounted for his ivory, so there is no way of getting at him on that issue.

wandering trader This refers to the man in patches Marlow meets on the bank.

Each station . . . The manager is contemptuous of Kurtz's idealism, and there is something to be said for his attitude, in view of what happens to Kurtz – not much, though: he is himself cynical, self-righteous and ambitious.

trust to this Ironic: shortly afterwards the uncle and his expedition vanish into the forest for ever.

sunlit . . . evil These words echo the image on p.28, as Marlow describes the shining Thames darkening.

less valuable animals i.e. men.

the surface, the reality Marlow prefers *not* to see the inner truth, clinging instead to superficial reality. This is a reversal of the usual quest theme, in which the seeker wishes to penetrate the surface of things to the core of truth and meaning.

the heart of darkness Marlow uses the phrase quite self-consciously: it is, of course, his consciousness of the symbolism which constitutes the substance of the story, as he tries to fathom what it means.

prehistoric This word evokes the very opening of the story. The Europeans come to Africa as the Romans came to Britain.

remote kinship This is a vital discovery for Marlow, and it leads him to the insight that 'Principles won't do.' What is needed – and this is one of Conrad's central convictions – is for the individual, as Marlow says, to 'meet that truth with his own true stuff – with his own inborn strength' rather than retreating behind a façade of 'principles' or simply avoiding the issue by concentrating on self-interest of one sort or another. The doctrine of 'meeting the truth' is the key to Marlow's regard for Kurtz who, for all the horrors of his life, has at least looked into the abyss and seen what there is to see – and that in spite of his own disabling high principles.

evil spirit To the natives, the steam-boat is another kind of devil in the European-made hell.

honest concern Another way of meeting the truth of the world's brute fact.

beautiful resignation Marlow's irony points to the way in which the manager acts a part.

screamed Once again the physical stillness and aural activity of the forest are sharply contrasted, as though it were a huge single body.

Winchesters Rifles.

Will they attack? The murmuring of the pilgrims matches the howling of the natives.

Eat 'im! Conrad heightens the comedy of this passage by making Marlow's language ('he and his chaps', 'of course', 'anyway') take on an especially low-key English quality in contrast with the fierce brusque words of the cannibals.

unappetizing Here the comedy becomes fantastic.

an enchanted princess The phrase reminds us of the story's mythical qualities: Marlow is a knight in quest of a mystery, situated in a dark wood.

eyes were in it Again we have the sense that the forest is a single creature. A few lines later Marlow says of the action that 'It developed itself . . .' All these allusions hint at a reversal of the expected order: the Europeans have turned the natives into things, by killing them with work, but the largest 'thing' of all – the encompassing forest – is itself alive. On p.79 it is given a face; a few lines earlier the river is said to have something like a backbone.

scow Flat-bottomed boat.

Martini-Henry A rifle designed by Messrs. Martini and Henry.

an understandable language The idea here recurs throughout the story: the naval manual is marked in mysterious cypher, the natives speak in unknown tongues, Marlow, like Kurtz himself, becomes just a voice in the darkness describing the incomprehensible. All point to the inadequacy of language or to the difficulty of understanding what is being said. Given that Kurtz's gift is for speech, we have the sense that there is ultimately nothing to be said; or, more exactly, that there is nothing ultimate speech can usefully express. The only route of escape is into action, work, daily labour. That is what Marlow opposes to speech. Yet he himself is a skilful story teller. The paradox remains.

doing . . . discoursing See note above. A few lines later the gift of expression is described as both a stream of light and a flow from the heart of darkness.

disinterred The word suggests how emaciated Kurtz already is, even before death.

utter solitude without a policeman This phrase, both comic and profoundly serious, sums up the situation.

initiated i.e. into the mystery of darkness.

exotic ... Benevolence The words evoke both the grandeur and the utter vagueness of the situation.

Exterminate all the brutes! Personally, I find this unconvincing and overstated.

he had done something ... The theme of work again. Something has been achieved amidst the chaos.

scandalized murmur ... Again the pilgrims match the noise on the bank. By describing them like magpies Marlow makes clear the parallel: one party is no more savage or civilized than the other, except in superficial matters. This section is full of sounds: howls, murmurs, muttering.

harlequin A pantomime character, sometimes in many-coloured clothes. The word also anticipates the wide-eyed, comic quality of the man in patches.

holland Coarse, unbleached linen.

talked and talked The patched man is a kind of parody of Kurtz. He chatters and gabbles.

Revision questions on Chapter 2

1 Why is Marlow so impressed by the naval manual, and what does his reaction tell us about his character?

2 Comment on the use of devil imagery. What is its purpose in this chapter?

3 What does Marlow feel about the forest on the banks and how are his feelings conveyed?

4 Why does Kurtz become so important to Marlow during the course of this chapter?

5 Comment on any unusual narrative techniques Conrad uses to develop the story.

Chapter 3

The man in patches gives an account of Kurtz's illness and his disturbing power over the natives. He also explains his own tricky relationship with Kurtz, who then appears carried on a stretcher, surrounded by groups of natives. At a sign from him, the natives disperse, and he is carried to the boat, accompanied by various 'pilgrims' and the manager. On board he is virtually a prisoner but manages to escape while the others are sleeping. Marlow follows Kurtz and finds him apparently taking part in a native ceremony. Marlow takes him back to the boat where he falls into intermittent delirium, dying a few days later after entrusting his private papers to Marlow's care. Marlow himself goes down with a near fatal fever. When recovered, he returns to Brussels to visit Kurtz's fiancée. She still believes in Kurtz as a great and good man, and Marlow has not the heart to tell her anything different. Instead, he claims that her name was the last sound on Kurtz's lips. The story ends, where it began, in the London twilight on board the *Nellie*.

Commentary

In a comic novel this might be called the concluding chapter in which nothing is concluded: the traditional pattern of the imperial adventure story is defeated, just as Marlow is defeated by the problems he has encountered. Nothing is solved, and the last paragraph refers us back to the book's opening doubts, as the Intended's 'certainty' is sharply contrasted with Marlow's doubt. In his earlier words, the outcome is 'not very clear'.

As if to emphasize this point the chapter's central events – Marlow's meetings with Kurtz – are narrated in a curiously muffled way. They have to be read carefully, if only to follow what passes between the two men – let alone what Marlow makes of it or what it means. Here, more than anywhere in the novella, what matters is what is not articulated but only implied. Judgements vary about Conrad's success in conveying his point. Many readers believe that by constantly evading the issue of the horrors Marlow sees – for example – Conrad fatally weakens the story. Others suggest that this successfully deflects our attention to its proper object: Marlow's state of mind. It is up to each reader to make up his or her mind. What can be said with confidence is that this is the crucial chapter in which the meaning of Marlow's experience is confronted, if only obliquely, and the real nature of Kurtz's activities is revealed. What is not clear is what we are to make of them. Is Kurtz a mad, evil man? A good man who has taken the wrong turning? A brave man who has faced up to the reality of life's ultimate meaninglessness and acted accordingly? A man who has fallen victim to the terrors of the wilderness? The point here is that Marlow simply does not know: he can only speculate, and his speculations are coloured by his earlier experiences with other employees of the Company. Compared with their pettiness and self-seeking, Kurtz, however disturbing his involvement in native rites and savage cruelty, has at least engaged with the fundamental nature of the country he lives in: he has not stood back and simply exploited it – through he *has* found more ivory than any other agent, and that seriously compromises any positive view we take of his career. Just as Kurtz himself has made a judgement, it is left to each reader to make a judgement on him.

glamour A favourite Conrad word – occurring often in *Lord Jim*, for example, and especially associated with youth. It is worth comparing this description of the patched man (p.93) with our various introductions to Kurtz, comparably driven to his jungle life. Marlow even suggests that while the man talks one forgets him. When Kurtz talks the hearer thinks of nothing else – and Kurtz ends by talking *only* of himself.

had found him out The situation of a man discovering himself in solitude and finding the discovery unbearable is a favourite Conrad device. The most famous example occurs in *Nostromo* when Decoud, stranded alone on an island, finally commits suicide.

crawl... Yet Marlow himself has spoken of crawling towards Kurtz (p.68), though in a rather different sense.

His voice...rustle Compare this passage with the descriptions of the Thames at the opening of the book.

She came abreast... We inevitably compare the two women in Kurtz's life: his Intended and this magnificent native – both lofty, dignified, theatrical.

a vapour exhaled This is the most explicit of many hints uniting Kurtz with the landscape, as though he has become the expression of what he set out to control. Two pages later the ebbing of Kurtz's life is connected with the flowing of the river down to the sea.

wring your heart... These words connect Kurtz, Marlow and Africa in a complex relationship. Both men have seen something – the core of the mystery – but neither can cope with it. This 'heart' is beyond control or expression.

The horror! This remains intentionally vague.

unexpressed depths Even the manager's meanness becomes a kind of mystery in this context. He is, as someone once said in another context, filled with emptiness.

something to say This is on a par with having something to *do*. In this paragraph Marlow offers his judgement of Kurtz, in which the horror he caused is balanced against the horror he perceived.

trespassed upon my thoughts Here Marlow himself is starting to become a Kurtz. He has looked into the abyss and it is beginning to affect him.

a great musician By a curious irony, this passage suggests the name of Albert Schweitzer (1875–1964) a great French organist and doctor, who devoted his life to an African medical settlement. Some thought of him as a saint; others saw him as a selfish autocrat who used his hospital to glorify his own name. The truth of the matter is unclear.

sunlight . . . lie This point picks up the many moments in the story when light is shown to be as sinister as darkness – and more deceptive, precisely because it *conceals* the residual darkness.

dusk was falling We return to the setting of the opening, but in a very different mood.

a lofty drawing-room Compare this with the drawing room of Marlow's aunt, and note the careful distinction made between them.

triumphant darkness This refers to the delusions the Intended insists on.

His words will remain Marlow speaks with conscious irony here.

tragic . . . Shade Just as we are invited to compare the Intended in her world of dreams with Marlow's aunt, so here we compare her with Kurtz's black mistress. On both he has had the same effect.

your name Marlow cannot bring himself to tell her the truth – so strong is the power of illusion and the world of ideals. But the question remains: does it matter that Marlow tells a lie here?

Revision questions on Chapter 3

1 What are Marlow's reasons for not telling the Intended the truth about Kurtz?

2 Give an account of the Patched Man's character and explain why he is so impressed by Kurtz.

3 What does Kurtz refer to when he says 'The Horror! The Horror!'?

4 What is the Manager's attitude to Kurtz?

5 What does Marlow learn from his meeting with Kurtz?

Conrad's art in *Heart of Darkness*
The characters

There are only two characters who really count in the book, insofar as characters are important at all: Marlow and Kurtz. They make a kind of symmetry which is so strong that we may lose sight of character in the normal fictional sense – highly differentiated individuals described in physical and mental detail – when we become involved in the shadowy interplay between them. At one moment Kurtz and Marlow seem far apart, at the next they are close together; and the relationship between them is not so much an encounter between two men, as between two metaphysical entities, two embodiments of good and evil. Yet even to say that is to draw a stronger line between them than the text justifies. Their attitudes to one another change by the minute, at times inexplicably, and we cannot be absolutely sure that the good and evil are so clearly distinguished between them.

The other characters in the novella, all sharply drawn, are much easier to recognize, escaping as they do from the confusing penumbra of Marlow's obsession with Kurtz and Kurtz's obsession with himself; and they give the book strong roots in a conventionally depicted reality, which sometimes makes the portentous mysticism of the Marlow/Kurtz relationship all the harder to take. This raises problems about how we are to read the text. Is it a realistic story in the nineteenth-century tradition? Is it a kind of morality tale? Or a psychodrama of the inner life? Or an allegory? Or some curious combination of all these? The problem is discussed in the commentaries, but it should be borne in mind when thinking about the characters and how they are presented, because there appear to be conflicting conventions of presentation in the text. This is not uncommon in novels, where more attention is naturally given to some characters than others, resulting in the two-tier effect noted long ago by E. M. Forster in *Aspects of the Novel* (1927). Forster comments on the difference between round and flat characters – the round ones, presented in greater detail and appearing to have 'depth', the flat resembling caricatures or types. That distinction isn't really adequate to what happens in *Heart of Darkness*, though it does admirably cover such individuals as the aunt and the Chief Accountant, flat characters who contribute to the story's black comedy; but it reminds us not to make assumptions about characterization in fiction. The description we might want to make in Conrad's book is between, let us say, sharp and vague – Kurtz and Marlow belonging to the second category. It is not so much depth the major characters have as uncertainty, mistiness, lack of outline, and this can be intriguing or disappointing according to the ways in which one reads the story. It is only fair to say that many readers have found Kurtz an anticlimax after the build-up he is given by Marlow, and the critical reader needs to think carefully about whether this is deliberate or accidental on Conrad's part. Does it add to the story or detract from it?

Marlow

The degree to which Marlow is a distinct character and the degree to which he is a substitute narrator for Conrad himself, allowing the novelist to stand at an ironic distance from his story while still embodying substantial aspects of his own character, can never be determined. Marlow shares certain obvious biographical circumstances with his creator: both were sailors, both worked in the Congo and the Malay archipelago, where several of the 'Marlow' stories are set, and both have a super-subtle gift for story-telling. On the other hand, Marlow is inclined to present himself as a simple chap, puzzled by the scenes he witnesses, which certainly cannot be said of Conrad himself. Perhaps the problem of identification between author and narrator can be clarified a little if we remember the importance of distinguishing role and character, the first determined by one's relations to others, the second a matter of individual traits and characteristics. Of course, the two cannot be entirely separated: the role we play in life is partly determined by our character, and vice versa; but it *is* possible to make a useful distinction when discussing literature. In these terms, Marlow's role is rather more important than his character. His function is to serve as a consciousness through which the events of the story are at once filtered and interpreted, but also given a depth and significance they would not otherwise have. In *Lord Jim* (1900) for example – the longest of the Marlow stories – the narrator plays a number of roles, assembling information, following up a story which would otherwise be lost in the obscurity of the Malayan islands, interpreting Jim's motives. The central character is a man painfully lacking in powers of self-expression: Marlow not only interprets his story to us, but also to Jim himself. Yet at the end, Conrad uses Marlow to imply that, however much has been understood, the whole thing remains wrapped in an ultimate mystery, and he is able to do this because he does not tell the story himself. A novelist, after all, is like God: he knows everything about his characters there is to know. This is not true of characters within the book: Marlow's very limitation, therefore – simply being one of the characters, not an omniscient narrator – is his strength, when it comes to conveying Conrad's vision of life as an ultimately baffling business. This point is obviously of major importance in *Heart of Darkness*, a narrative in which the story-teller's successful completion of his quest in search of Kurtz only deepens the mystery. Kurtz is apparently the opposite of Lord Jim – the epitome of eloquence; but this only intensifies the irony when Kurtz's magnificent language is seen to conceal a hollowness which is itself the strangest enigma of all, as though Kurtz's power issued not from what he possessed but from what he lacked.

This is the enigma Marlow has to wrestle with in the latter part of the story, and Conrad is careful to set up the character appropriately. At the beginning of the book, the audience – Director of Companies, Lawyer, Accountant, and Conrad himself – are all introduced by a few words, though Conrad restricts his own appearance to simply setting the scene; Marlow, on the other hand, speaks before he is introduced – and speaks very dramatically. Vividly, out of the calm silence, come portentous words:

'And this also,' said Marlow suddenly, 'has been one of the dark places of the earth.'

This provides a keynote for the man, the subject of the story, and one of its main motifs. Marlow clearly has a sense of the theatrical – a sense amply developed in the rest of the story: he knows how to make an effect, which is a major part of story-telling, and in this respect he is a true representative of his creator. In one ominous sentence he refers to what is to come i.e. the linking of the dark continent with the darkness of Europe and the darkness in men's souls. He also alerts us to the power of the human voice, especially in darkness, which is to play such an important part in the subsequent narrative; for here, Marlow speaks impressively out of the twilight with all the eloquence for which Kurtz is famed. On the next page we are told that:

'His remark did not seem at all surprising. It was just like Marlow.'

He already has a reputation for oracular pronouncements, tale-telling and mysteries. This is important, for the activity of putting words together effectively is a preoccupation here and elsewhere in

Conrad. Marlow himself returns to the topic again and again in *Heart of Darkness*, usually in the form of a contrast between the blessedness of work and action and the disturbing, unsettling power of thought and its medium, language. Kurtz is a fascinating, powerful man, precisely because he seems able to forge a link between the two, to make words give rise to action. Marlow, on the other hand, can only bring the two together by telling stories *about* actions. Otherwise, he immerses himself in mundane tasks to avoid the introspection to which he is too much inclined, and which, if indulged, would destroy the power to act entirely. But introspection – the activity of looking into oneself – is closely connected with imagination – the power of creating what does not already exist – and imagination is itself a source of action: exploration, for example, and invention. So it is ultimately impossible to separate imagination, introspection and action, words and deeds, and this is Marlow's dilemma. He desires to be purely a man of action, but he is, willy-nilly, also a man of imagination.

Unlike his audience, Marlow is still a sailor, but he is also, as Conrad puts it, a wanderer (p.29), and the two activities are as different yet as closely linked as action and imagination. Sailors are inclined to cultivate a domesticated simplicity, to regard the rest of the world outside their ships as a straightforward place, not worth much attention. Marlow is the very reverse of this: like his creator, he has a subtle sense for the hidden significance of things – hidden not *within* them but, as it were, fleetingly glimpsed by those with eyes to see. In a crucial passage Conrad puts it like this:

'to him the meaning of an episode was not inside, like a kernel but outside, enveloping the tale which brought it out only as a glow brings out a haze, in the likeness of one of those misty haloes that sometimes are made visible by the spectral illumination of moonshine.'

The language here – haze, likeness, misty, spectral – makes a vital point about the story we are soon to hear: not only that its significance is apparent to Marlow alone, but that this significance is doubtful and impalpable – there is nothing certain about it. What is going to matter for the reader is what Marlow *makes* of the situation, not what it unambiguously is. There is a sense, therefore, in which Marlow is a teller of tall tales: fantastic fictions which we may choose to believe or not, for there is no way of proving them. That is the doubt which remains at the end of the story. As Conrad puts it (p.32):

'. . . we knew we were fated, before the ebb began to run, to hear one of Marlow's inconclusive experiences.'

Which is not to say that the story Marlow tells is at all loose-limbed or ill-focused. On the contrary, Conrad gives him a talent for sharp, grotesque characterization, for widely varying the pace of the narrative, and for setting it in a vivid context, both historically and immediately. For such a comparatively short novella – 38,000 words – there is an extraordinary amount of description, reflection and detail. Only the core of the story and its meaning are indistinct, for reasons discussed elsewhere (see the character of Kurtz). But it is the very vividness of the settings and minor characters which makes the final effect puzzling: having raised our expectations, by the clarity and strength of its discourse, the tale dashes them all the more remarkably when it declines without an equally clear and strong conclusion. Argument among readers has raged as to whether this is a virtue or a vice on Conrad's part – as to whether the uncertainty is a part of Marlow's positive discovery or just a case of the author not knowing what to do with his story. Perhaps we should remember, at this point, that uncertainty and vagueness are not the same thing, and that though the *character* of Marlow may be left with a doubt, the *story* comes to a positive and ironic full-stop. And it is not Marlow who is vague, but the truth he is trying to grasp.

The complication here is caused by the difficulty of distinguishing exactly what the story is about. Are we primarily concerned with Kurtz's individual fate, with its larger significance, with the problem of colonialism, with the general evil in the heart of man, or with Marlow's personal discovery? At the beginning of his narrative, Marlow positively disclaims the last theme as his subject:

I don't want to bother you much with what happened to me personally.

Conrad comments, however, that this remark shows:

. . . the weakness of many tellers of tales who seem so often unaware of what their audience would best like to hear . . .

and it is clearly the case that Marlow plays a major role in the book, not only as the mediating consciousness through which the events are described, but as an individual who is affected by those events, which are in turn coloured by the way in which he narrates them. Marlow has made a discovery in his Congo adventure, and it is as much that discovery he is trying to clarify when telling the tale, as the tale itself. In a certain sense, the discovery *is* the tale. Considered objectively the contents of the story – like so many great stories – are thin enough. As I suggest in the section on plot (see pp.13–15), there is hardly any substance to what Marlow narrates: a rather sordid trip up a horrible river accompanied by petty intrigues and concluded with the removal of a sick agent who may be mad. What matters, as Marlow himself says, is that the episode represents:

... the culminating point of my experience. It seemed to throw a kind of light on everything about me – and into my thoughts.

The irony here, of course, is that the *light* is thrown by *darkness*, and that what it illuminates is itself a further darkness. As he comments:

It was ... not very clear, either. No, not very clear.

Even his motives for pursuing the experience in the first place are cloaked in mystery. He tells us about his boyhood desire to explore the blank places on the map, which has survived into maturity, though the spaces are now filled, and even the great empty expanse of Central Africa has become 'a place of darkness' i.e. one no longer filled with the light of childhood dreams. At this stage 'darkness' already signifies knowledge: what was unknown is now superficially known. It is only after his experience that he realizes that the darkness goes much deeper, and that personal knowledge is indeed exactly what reveals it. But this raises the question: is the revealed darkness in the place or the person who visits it? Does *it* not discover darkness in *them*? And that is the question Marlow confronts.

Kurtz

Kurtz is most remarkable in the first part of the story by his absence, and then by the increasingly frequent mention of his name before we ever meet him. First mentioned on p.20 of a 90 page story, he appears only 22 pages before the end, when he is already mortally ill. Few of his words are reported directly, and only with the closest concentration can the reader follow his few physical appearances. What really matters about Kurtz is the effect he has on others, like a stone which has already disappeared below the pond's surface though the ripples stretch out for yards. Even Marlow, the character most affected, experiences Kurtz mostly at second-hand, through the reports of others, and his own encounters with the man are strangely inconclusive, convincing him at one moment that the man is evil, at another that he is not, at yet another that he is mad. We first hear of him from the prim and proper Chief Accountant, who tells Marlow that Kurtz is a first-class agent and 'a very remarkable person' – chiefly, it seems, because he sends in more ivory than all the other agents put together. His trading-post is in the deepest interior, but the Accountant believes that, in time, Kurtz will be 'somebody' in the European administration of the Company. This view is shared by both his admirers and his enemies, as we learn later, when we overhear a conversation between the manager and his nephew, and when Marlow talks to the Chief Brickmaker. What we also learn from the Chief Accountant's words – indirectly – is that the local Company staff are in awe of Kurtz, and possibly afraid of him. The Accountant wishes him to know, via Marlow, that everything is satisfactory at his end; the Manager resents Kurtz's influence; the patched man is completely under his thumb. A few pages later, Marlow meets the Manager, who praises Kurtz in the highest terms, yet we soon learn how much he is hated; it seems that hypocrisy affects more than the European treatment of natives, infecting the internal relationships in the Company. Kurtz is thus presented from the start as a focus for the best and worst feelings of the other characters; and as a way of showing the complex relationship between those feelings, when they become part of a power struggle.

This complexity is vividly illustrated a few pages later by Marlow's talk with the Chief Brickmaker, prefaced by the description of a painting, the work of Kurtz himself, which hangs in the brickmaker's room. The painting sets against a sombre background the figure of a woman: 'draped and blindfolded, carrying a lighted torch'. In view of what he says about Kurtz, it is unclear why the brickmaker has the picture in his room at all – perhaps to curry favour. The painting itself is ambiguous. Justice is traditionally represented by a blindfolded woman, and the torch would seem to symbolize enlightenment – but the figure is set against an 'almost black' background, and the effect of the torchlight on the woman's face is described by Marlow as sinister. The image of the torch against darkness which it does not pierce reminds us of Marlow's earlier claim that his voyage threw 'a kind of light' which served only to reveal a lack of clarity. The picture thus serves to symbolize his plight; but it also throws its own light on Kurtz who, according to the brickmaker, is associated with the 'gang of virtue' – to which

Marlow also belongs, because of his European recommendation. Having inveighed against this new dispensation, however, the brickmaker is careful to tell Marlow that he has, of course, the highest respect for Kurtz etc. Thus already we can see the disturbing effect Kurtz has on everyone around him: he has become the cause of lying and hypocrisy in his fellow workers, just as he is to be the object of 'unspeakable rites' among his African followers. And all this flows from his lofty reputation and high-minded motives.

Yet almost more important than the effects Kurtz has on his fellows, is the way in which he literally stimulates Marlow's imagination. Because the man is only 'a word' to him at this stage, Marlow begins to picture possible situations. On p.64 he:

'seemed to see Kurtz for the first time. It was a distinct glimpse: the dugout, four paddling savages, and the lone white man turning his back suddenly on the headquarters, on relief, on thoughts of home . . .'

Marlow has this vision while lying concealed on his boat, listening to the Manager and his uncle discussing 'that man', and he has as yet no direct knowledge of Kurtz. The association of Kurtz in Marlow's mind with an imaginative vision – even such a simple visual image as this – is a major clue to the drift of the whole story, which persistently points to Kurtz as a man with power, for better or worse, over men's minds and hearts. That 'for better or worse' is also important: the ambiguous nature of power – its capacity to ruin or to save – is a subordinate theme of the story. As he goes further up the river, Marlow becomes especially vulnerable to visions of Kurtz, as he finds his sense of reality under attack (see especially p.67), and becomes more and more preoccupied with dreams:

'It seems to me I am trying to tell you a dream . . . the very essence of dreams' (p.57)

As reality fades, but the 'inner truth' remains hidden, so dreams – or rather, nightmares – take over; and it is with dreams, nightmares and visions that Marlow associates Kurtz. At the same time, Kurtz becomes identified in his mind with the landscape through which he is travelling: 'The earth seemed unearthly' (p.69) he tells us, just before they get to the Inner Station; and when they find the Patched Man's naval manual, he exclaims on: 'the delicious sensation of having come upon something unmistakably real . . .' (p.71) though even this reality has the mystery of the cypher attached to it. By now Marlow is thinking of the journey in terms of Kurtz, not the Station, as its objective; and the approach is:

'beset by as many dangers as though he had been an enchanted princess sleeping in a fabulous castle' (p.77)

which is both apt and comically grotesque when one thinks of the man and the setting. Two final features of the journey underline the dreamy atmosphere: the thick fog which descends and rises in moments, and the abrupt way in which the steamer comes upon the Inner Station, almost by mistake when the party have ceased to look for it. By now Marlow imagines himself listening to Kurtz's voice, so frustrated is he by the possibility they will never reach him, and the narrative becomes confused, mixing present, past and future events. Even when they reach the Station, Marlow's encounter with Kurtz is still delayed, this time by the Patched Man, who provides yet another perspective on the dying agent.

All this time Kurtz's biography is built up in fragments from various sources: the Chief Accountant, the Manager, the Chief Brickmaker, the Patched Man; and by direct narrative when (pp.84–7) in a kind of semi-delirium, Marlow brings together facts he learns after Kurtz's death, and after his own return to Europe, with what he already knows. Then, in a series of shocks, the narrative brings home to Marlow the ramifications of Kurtz's position. First, he catches sight of the shrunken head through his binoculars (p.96); then Kurtz suddenly appears on a stretcher (p.98) as if rising up out of the ground (echoing the phrase 'disinterred body'). Next the magnificent native woman appears on the bank (p.101). Finally, Kurtz has to be retrieved again from some strange rite in which he is taking part (106). Again and again the imagery of the grave recurs: Kurtz is as though already dead, he is 'like a vapour exhaled by the earth' (106), he is 'like an animated image of death' (99). The significance of these references is clear enough, and Kurtz's association with death might be the final judgement on him, were Marlow to dig no deeper: not for nothing does he describe Kurtz as 'the nightmare of my choice' (p.105), for by encountering him only when he is dying, Marlow is given an insight into the profoundest issues of life and death. It is this insight he struggles to interpret, as though Kurtz were a messenger from beyond the grave. For balanced against the horror – the shrunken heads, the threats, the impalpable sense of evil – there is also the adoration of the natives, of the Patched Man, and of the Intended; and there is Marlow's own admiration, in spite of himself, of a man who:

'. . . had something to say. He said it . . . He had summed up – he had judged.' (p113).

Kurtz is not a good man, but he is a remarkable one: in this discovery, Marlow transcends all the conventions of the nineteenth-century realistic novel which demand that the 'hero' should be, if not unimpeachable, at least human. But Kurtz is in the long line of monsters and anti-heroes – Frankenstein's monster, Mr Rochester, Heathcliff – who seem to go beyond the 'merely' human. Indeed, Marlow and Kurtz are not unlike Henry Frankenstein and his creation: drawn to one another yet utterly opposite. Both look into the abyss and find life meaningless, but Marlow has to live on with this knowledge: 'I remained to dream the nightmare out to the end.' (p.112) Indeed, Marlow almost envies Kurtz, for although the man has died with the famous words – 'The horror! The horror!' – on his lips, this is at least, as Marlow puts it, 'the expression of some sort of belief' (p.113). Unable to believe in the noble causes he started out with, Kurtz has not retreated into a twilight zone of faith in nothing but mere existence: instead he has worshipped the devil of himself, when the god of virtue fails him. This is, in Marlow's words:

'. . . an affirmation, a moral victory, paid for by innumerable defeats, by abominable terrors, by abominable satisfactions. But it was a victory! That is why I have remained loyal to Kurtz . . .' (p.113).

So strong is Kurtz that he continues to exert influence, even after death, on Marlow and on the Intended. Yet even then, his identity remains uncertain. His cousin describes him as a musician, and a journalist friend as a politician. The Intended continues to see him as an heroic visionary. But the strangest testimony to his strength comes from Marlow himself:

I had a vision of him on the stretcher, opening his mouth voraciously, as if to devour all the earth with all its mankind. He lived then before me; he lived as much as he had ever lived . . . The vision seemed to enter the house with me . . . It was a moment of triumph for the wilderness . . .' (p.116)

The contrast with the description of the Intended which follows almost immediately could hardly be more remarkable, and constitutes the final irony of the book.

Minor characters

A surprisingly wide range of minor characters make their appearance in the story, all playing significant small parts, and all carefully distinguished. The aunt, the doctor, the Belgian clerk, the Swedish captain, the Chief Accountant, Marlow's companion on his jungle trek, the Manager, the Manager's uncle, the Chief Brickmaker, the Chief Engineer, the Helmsman, the Patched Man, the Intended, Kurtz's black mistress, the Manager's boy, and – of course – the cannibals aboard the boat, the pilgrims, Marlow's audience, and the natives on shore: quite an impressive cast for a story of 38,000 words. However brief his or her appearance, each one is particularized by a phrase or trait – such as the clerk's slang, and his chin 'shaped like the toe of an old boot' (p.37). Even the old ladies in the Company office in Brussels are carefully described, and individuals among the cannibals, the natives and the pilgrims are picked out from the crowd. All this helps to give the story its air of verisimilitude: the sheer density and proliferation of detail involves us in a belief in the story, highlighting the curious shadows at its heart.

Of the minor characters the four most developed are the Manager, the Chief Brickmaker, the Patched Man and the Intended.

The Manager

Based on an agent Conrad himself encountered during his own trip up the Congo, this character represents his revenge on a man who treated him badly. The initial description of his character and behaviour is hardly pleasing; commonplace (the word 'common' appears three times in different forms, and he is also said to be 'ordinary'), stealthy, uneasy and inspiring unease, without learning, intelligence, initiative or organizational power, his only virtues – if they can even be called such – are a powerful gaze and superlative health. The man has his position, simply by virtue of outlasting all those of weaker constitution. Marlow's judgement is harsh, perhaps a little too harsh: the invention of the round table is, after all, a witty solution to a difficult problem; but its harshness is not related merely to Conrad's personal bitterness, but to the far more important issue – within the story – of the manager's behaviour towards Kurtz. Marlow is careful to emphasize his hypocrisy: behaving at all times with formal correctness in public, the Manager is privately eager to see an obstacle to his own promotion out of the way, and his motives are known to Marlow, who overhears the conversation between his enemy and his enemy's uncle (pp.63–5). But the conflict runs deeper still, for the opening description of the manager is used to establish the complete antithesis between his nature and Kurtz's. The Manager is always correct, and never knowingly or consciously does wrong, although he wills it with all the strength of his nature, and rejoices in the other man's downfall when it comes. Technically, he is virtuous, where Kurtz is evil; but the story reveals Marlow's perplexing discovery that Kurtz's evil, horrifying though it is, has at least the redeeming qualities of grandeur, vision and fulfilment. Kurtz rises above the petty, commonplace observances which constitute the nullity of his enemy's life, into a realm quite beyond his comprehension. Above all, he faces up to the emptiness at the heart of darkness — the horror — which the Manager's life embodies without acknowledging. Kurtz, it might be said, takes responsibility for his sins; the Manager does not.

The Chief Brickmaker

This character, humorously dubbed 'the brickmaker of the Central Station' by Marlow, is carefully contrasted to the Manager, though he, too, is envious of Kurtz as the new dispensation he appears to represent. Aristocratic and distinguished, where the Manager is commonplace and vulgar, he is openly cynical where the Manager is circumspect. Yet even he is frightened of Kurtz. Calling him a 'papier mâché Mephistopheles', Marlow discovers that the Brickmaker is, in his way, as squalid as the Manager; and by letting him talk on, Marlow also makes the disturbing discovery that he is being manipulated by the image of Kurtz into telling a virtual lie, even before he has met the man (p.57). The pettiness of the pilgrims has already disposed him in favour of the Inner Station's agent. So the Brickmaker, like the Manager, fulfills a vital role in turning Marlow's mind towards Kurtz, which means that, even when he encounters the horrors of Kurtz's rule in the jungle, he is still inclined to look for what is good in the dying man's behaviour, and almost anything is better than the 'flabby, pretending, weak-eyed devil' (p.43) who tempts the pilgrims and their like.

The Patched Man

Designated as a harlequin, the Patched Man has more than a little of the clown about him. Russian in origin, he is distantly related to that common character in nineteenth-century Russian literature, the holy fool: the simpleton or idiot who ultimately proves to be wiser about life than the clever or sophisticated people around him. The extent of the Patched Man's wisdom about Kurtz is doubted by Marlow, who believes that his devotion to the dying man is:

'... about the most dangerous thing in every way he had come upon so far' (p.94)

The dangerous route to wisdom is not necessarily the worst, however: the Patched Man's simplicity and innocence contrast vividly with the petty self-seeking of the pilgrims, *and* with the horror experienced by Kurtz. He seems to exemplify perfectly Marlow's doctrine that salvation is of the surface, to be found in the day's work and a preoccupation with the simple tasks of life. This is expressed in his delight at recovering the naval manual which Marlow has earlier described (p.71) as:

'Not a very enthralling book; but at the first glance you could see there a singleness of intention, an honest concern for the right way of going to work ... something unmistakably real.'

It is the sense of something 'unmistakably real' which the Patched Man kept despite his months of extraordinary wandering in the jungle – and it is just this sense which everyone else seems to lose, above all, Kurtz himself. Typically, the 'mystery' of the cipher has a simple solution: the characters are simply Russian letters, and there *is* no mystery. Everything about the Patched Man is of the surface.

This makes his response to Kurtz all the more interesting. A simple man himself (and that, of course, is a good thing in Marlow's book) he is impressed by Kurtz's profundity, his cleverness, his imagination, his eloquence – all the things for which he is famous, and which Marlow comes so seriously to doubt. In a sense, Kurtz and the Patched Man are very close. The Patched Man is driven on by glamour, he is ruled by the pure spirit of adventure, and this gives him a grandeur which we may compare with Kurtz. The difference – and it is a vital one – is that the Patched Man is entirely without self-interest or material desires: where Kurtz has succumbed to the temptations of success and the desire to exercise power, the Patched Man is completely uncorrupted. He actually prefers to be without worldly possessions, to live unknown in the jungle, to endure privations. He is, in fact, the embodiment of a simple, passionate, almost Franciscan goodness, and the nearest we come in this story to the sense that the world may not be entirely a place of horror. He senses that Kurtz has gone further into things than he has – but the point of the story, insofar as it has one, is to suggest that 'going into things' may not be such a good idea: it produces the courage and unflinching vision Marlow attributes to Kurtz – 'He had summed up – he had judged' – but the vision is terrifyingly nihilistic. Kurtz's admirers are right to believe in his spirituality – but Conrad shows us that spirituality may itself be the most dangerous, the most destructive power there is, when it reveals the emptiness at the heart of things. The Patched Man is, in this sense, completely *un*spiritual, but far closer to one traditional view of Christianity, in that he has freed himself from the desires – grand and trivial – which beset the other characters.

The Intended

The remarkable portrait, saved for the end of the novella, though hinted at once earlier (p.84) at one level balances Marlow's aunt at the book's opening, but it is also more significant, for it consummates the novella's powerful irony in a final scene of complete misunderstanding. The scene is carefully set in the story's habitual dusk which fills the grand drawing-room just as it filled the forest, and the description of the Intended invites us to compare her with Kurtz's native mistress – an invitation which is made explicit on p.120.

'She put out her arms . . . a tragic and familiar Shade, resembling in this gesture another one, tragic also, and bedecked with powerless charms, stretching bare brown arms over the glitter of the infernal stream . . .'

Despite her wealthy surroundings, the girl has affinities with the Patched Man: Kurtz has profoundly influenced both, and both associate him especially with the idea of love, personal and general. Like the Patched Man, she has a kind of innocence: Marlow sees her as: 'guileless, profound, confident and trustful . . .' (p.117). And he is forced to wonder whether she, like the Patched Man, though wrong about Kurtz, has not acquired in consequence, 'a great and saving illusion' (p.119). For Kurtz, like the wilderness with which Marlow identifies him, has the faculty of eliciting from others whatever is in their deepest nature, bringing out the native pettiness of the Manager and Brickmaker, while creating scope for the tenderness and goodness of the Patched Man and the Intended. Marlow learns that even if the object of that tenderness and goodness is unworthy of them, the power of producing them is nevertheless a power to be respected. This is among his reasons – of which, perhaps, embarrassment is the strongest – for lying to the girl about Kurtz's last words. Doing an injustice to Kurtz, in the sense that he lies about the dead man's final vision, he does him justice in another way by preserving intact the memory which is so important to his former fiancée. Whether, in the long run, that memory will not destroy whatever other chance she has of a happy life, is an ironic question the story leaves unanswered.

Marlow's final confrontation is, in many ways, the finest thing in the book, for it highlights so very vividly the predicament his meeting with Kurtz has put him in. His notions of right and wrong, truth and falsehood, good and evil have blurred. Life is more puzzling than it was before he went up the Congo – a fact which is registered by the complexity of his feelings in the girl's presence. Her character, as such, is hardly developed. What matters is its impact on Marlow. The Intended embodies for him all the illusions, not only about Kurtz, but about the enterprise in which Kurtz was involved, and having discovered that superficial European notions about the distinction between the savage and the civilized are no longer adequate to his insights, he also understands that a simple correction of the girl's misunderstanding might only deepen his confusion – as it would certainly intensify her unhappiness. By taking away her illusion about Kurtz he would be removing the thing she lives by – and Marlow has discovered that 'civilized' life needs illusions or dreams, at the book's opening he calls them 'ideas' – if it is to survive at all. As to the question of whether it is worth saving – that is a problem too difficult to contemplate. This beautiful woman stands for everything European civilization has created – just as the native mistress seemed to embody the profoundest values of native culture. How is one to judge them? How is one to balance them against one another? How is one to say that one is more valuable than the other? Marlow has no answer to these questions, and therefore no right to destroy the girl's illusions.

Setting and themes

Setting

I have suggested that Africa — the principle setting — remains relatively indeterminate: though the three river stations are somewhat particularized, the continent beyond them — always threatening to reabsorb their flimsy structures in its encroaching chaos — remains unfocused. There is little to distinguish one part of the endless river and forest from another. This is certainly the case; yet there are also two ways in which Conrad does develop a sharper profile for the dark continent: in its relation to Europe, and in the forms European settlement takes, on the coast, and the banks of the Congo. The book begins and ends in Europe, just as it begins and ends in a kind of present. Although Conrad is narrating Marlow's story at second-hand, we have a sense at the end of returning to the story-teller's present, rather than to a remote past: this is reinforced by the sense of return from Africa to Europe where not only the story, but also the text began. The book thus has a kind of spatial and temporal symmetry, with Africa literally at its heart, in between two evocations of Europe; and just as the double narrative (Conrad retelling Marlow's story in Marlow's words) distances the events in time, so the setting seems to distance it into an ever deeper historical, or even extra-historical perspective. The sense of pre-history is explicitly evoked by Marlow at the beginning of his story, before the narrative proper begins. A parallel contrast and comparison is made between Europe and Africa, with the implication that this pre-history is still present just below the surface of 'civilized' life, just as Africa and Europe, for all their profound differences, are closer than we think, under the skin.

Europe is characterized in a number of ways, hinting at both the similarities and the contrasts with Africa. The maximum points of difference appear in the symmetrical descriptions of the two drawing-rooms at the beginning and end of the novel — one belonging to the narrator's aunt, the other to Kurtz's Intended. Each is described so as to fit the character and role of its occupant — the girl's lofty, aristocratic and gracious, even tragic; the aunt's mischievously and finally categorized simply as looking:

'most soothingly . . . just as you would expect a lady's drawing-room to look' (38)

which tells one everything about the complete conventionality of Marlow's aunt. Yet Conrad also makes it quite clear that the two rooms are meant to stand for more than individual characters: the very fact that each is representative of a certain class and attitude is enough to tell us that, but there is more to it. Both epitomize exactly that civilization, i.e. material refinement and comfort, which appears to be lacking in Africa, and which Marlow specifically links with his idea of European womanhood. The nineteenth-century drawing-room in a bourgeois or aristocratic house was essentially the woman's – one might more precisely say the *lady's* – domain; nothing could be more remote from the discomfort and uncertainty of the African forest. But Marlow goes further still, suggesting that this domain is not only materially comfortable, but intellectually and emotionally cosy, too. Both the aunt and the girl – the one comically, the other tragically – live in a world of their own. Marlow sees them as cut off from the real world, and he even suggests that this is typical of women in general: men are forced to live with facts, while women build castles in the air, remote from reality. Later in the novella, when we encounter Kurtz's superb African mistress – as we conclude her to be – we may cite her as evidence of Marlow's self-deception or misogyny; or, we may decide that his comment on all women is meant to apply only to European women, and in particular to that curious species known as 'the lady': the tragicomic creation of eighteenth- and nineteenth-century Europe. This figure was the object of satire from Pope to Jane Austen, from Dickens to Hardy, and the essence of the satire is that ladies must never, under any circumstances, be allowed to come into contact with unpleasant reality: when they do, they either deny its existence, retreat or change the subject. In general, however, reality has to be accommodated to their version of it. In this version, everything must be good, pleasant and nice, morally uplifting and shaped to expectations. This is the point Marlow makes in different ways about both his aunt and Kurtz's Intended.

But before we accuse Conrad of misogyny we should note that a world which produces *ladies* also requires *gentlemen* to go with them (mere men and women being servants, inferiors or natives); and they, too, play a part in the novel, in the forms of the Chief Accountant and the Manager. Both men are determined to get out of Africa what they want, and resolutely to ignore the reality of the place – a refusal aptly symbolized by their exquisite clothes and fastidious manners. In their way, the colonizers are as blind to reality as their female counterparts at home – and this says something about Europe's attitude to Africa in general: the two are as far apart as they could possibly be, and the Europeans intend to keep it that way. And this is true even of the more well-meaning among them: for if Africa is to remain exotic, exciting, remote, mysterious, it must remain as *different* from Europe as possible, and different, in this case, means primitive. So there is no need for the Europeans to make much even of their own settlements – no more, that is, than is necessary for achieving their purpose – getting out the ivory. The great causes of Civilization and Progress are bogus, as Marlow realizes early on, covers for a much more squalid activity. (For more on this see the discussion of Kurtz.) The Belgian settlements express a number of things about the Europeans – not only their attitude to Africa as an ultimately temporary trading post from which the maximum of profit must be extracted, but also their attitude to themselves and to their own culture. Marlow's trip to Brussels at the beginning of the book gives a strong hint of this. The city is a whited sepulchre, a monument to hypocrisy: at the very heart of their empire, the Belgians are deceiving themselves about its nature. It is run, after all, by a profit-making company, as the early British East Indian Empire was – not even by detached civil servants. The atmosphere of the company office is funereal and sinister, the company doctor is slightly dotty, and the young man who takes Marlow to the surgery is coarsely cynical. Only the heavily satirized aunt seems to believe in the higher purpose of the Company, and she obviously knows nothing about reality. Appropriately, all these features – cynicism, the sense of unreality, sinister drabness – can be found in the places Marlow visits on his journey down the river, and they are shown to affect most of the inhabitants with depression or even madness. At one level of the story we are shown that it is Africa which can make men mad; more profoundly, their insanity appears to be a virus they bring with them, which incubates in the silence and solitude of the jungle. For the Europeans Africa is like a dark mirror, which shows them what they are. The tatty trading posts and horrific mine workings are not produced by the miserable natives but by their Belgian masters, whose crime is compounded by the persistent delusion that Africa is a hell which they must endure, holding it, where possible, at arm's length, by perfect dressing or the maintenance of European manners. But the hell is one they have created, for themselves and for the natives. We sense that the colonizers, like Milton's Satan in *Paradise Lost*, make the inferno out of themselves, and out of their deepest desires.

And this last point is perhaps the profoundest locational motif of the story, the theme which runs from the first page to the last, uniting the two continents of Europe and Africa with the image of darkness and water. For a striking thing about the story is that it takes place almost entirely on rivers, although its essence is concerned with the exploration – and exploitation – of territories: Africa, the human heart, Europe. The story is *told* aboard a boat on the river which leads (in 1900, when the book was written) into the heart of world civilization, which also happened to be the centre of world trade and economic activity; while it largely occurs on board Marlow's rickety steamer travelling down the Congo, or at outposts so precariously based on the bank that they are almost more part of the water than the land. Even without Marlow's reflections on the obvious comparison between the darkness of the two continents, our eyes would therefore inevitably be focused on it, and the last words of the story make such a comparison quite explicit. The hell to which the story constantly refers, with its imagery of fiends and devils, and the mystery to which it points, are to be found as much in Europe as in Africa.

Themes

The prospect of trying to disentangle the themes in a book such as *Heart of Darkness* is a fearsome one. Although there are several points in the narrative at which Marlow states what he takes to be the meaning of his strange experience – and that is what forms the book's substance – he never says exactly the same thing twice. Take his attitude to Kurtz for example: equivocal is a mild way to describe it. While Kurtz himself has made a final judgement on existence – 'The horror! The horror!' – Marlow himself is unable to make a final judgement on Kurtz: he is both a remarkable man and an evil one, a visionary and a hollow demagogue, a self-deceiver and a confronter of the deepest truth about human life, according to Marlow at different stages of his encounter with the dying agent. Instead of stating a theme and developing it clearly, the book circles round and round the same points, viewing them from shifting perspectives. Sometimes these perspectives are so different that they appear to contradict one another or to be looking at different objects. Perhaps, then, we have to accept that ambiguity, uncertainty, doubt, evasiveness and transience are themselves 'themes' of the text: even though not always presented as such, they constitute much of the story's substance. It is not what Marlow experiences and narrates that matters, but what he *thinks* he has experienced and what he is often *unable* to narrate, but can only point to or imply. And at the very core of the book is an experience – his encounter with Kurtz – to which he cannot give a name because it has no parallel in his previous experience. It may even be – he implies – that the experience is intrinsically nameless: a sort of confrontation with Nothingness which resists all attempts to describe it.

Looking at the story in this way would suggest that it is a kind of allegory: the trip up the Congo stands for a spiritual journey into the heart of existence. There are plenty of hints to support such an interpretation. However, before dealing with this daunting theme, it can be said that the novella refers, directly or tangentially, to many other matters of topical interest when it was written. First and foremost, there is obviously the matter of colonization. European nations had been acquiring overseas empires for almost four centuries when Conrad wrote, but it was only during the later years of the nineteenth century that what became known as the 'Scramble for Africa' really got going; and it was only then that the colonizers began to give serious thought to what they saw as the moral and religious implications of an activity which had previously been seen largely in terms of trade. Of course missionaries had been sent out to South America and the Far East as early as the sixteenth century; and the nineteenth century saw the development of a serious debate in Britain which had by far the largest, oldest and best-run of the European empires, about the status of colonies. Already, by 1850 Lord Macaulay (1800–59) and the philosopher John Stuart Mill (1806–73) were insisting that imperial acquisitions could not be permanent: once the governing power had established a stable and humane system of education, trade and administration – which they saw as the legitimate purpose of empire – it was under an obligation to withdraw. This was quite a popular view in Britain, but inevitably, the men who stood to make vast amounts of money out of the colonies, and others who saw jobs for their children in the expanding administration and prosperity for the motherland in developing trade, took a different view. Like the Belgians in Conrad's novella, many pro-imperialists attempted to reconcile the two views, and to claim that not only did trade follow the flag: so did Christianity and civilization. What was good for trade was good for the soul. By the end of the century, with Queen Victoria's proclamation as Empress of India, and the increasing threat of imperial competition from France, Belgium, Italy and – most of all – Germany (soon to be at war with Britain), this view become more and more popular. It is immortalized – though not always espoused – in the stories of Kipling (1865–1931) and Haggard (1856–1925), where the White Man's Burden is celebrated.

There were many writers – Kipling, Forster and Conrad himself – who saw that the whole problem was far more complicated than this. Colonization was not simply a matter of dressing a lot of funny natives in proper underclothes and teaching them to pray to the Christian God: it often involved profoundly disturbing effects on the colonized country. Fifty years before Conrad wrote, Lord Macaulay had warned against the dangers of displacing the native culture in India – not only equal to Europe's, in his view, but in some respects superior. And besides the effect of colonization on the subject peoples there was also the question of what happened to the colonists themselves. They, too, were profoundly influenced by their presence in an alien culture, even when they thought themselves superior to that culture. This is one of Conrad's themes in *Heart of Darkness*, which shows how, while the natives are physically exploited and even destroyed by their colonial masters – who regard them as little more than animals – the Europeans suffer too: not at the hand of the natives but under the influence of the wilderness. What the inhabitants cannot do – resist the white man – their country does for them. Conrad, as I have suggested, develops this theme at the metaphysical level, describing the kind of spiritual death Kurtz undergoes, and which Marlow nearly suffers, too; on a simpler level he also shows us how the climate alone obliterates almost everyone who ventures into it. Because of the way in which the story is written, this physical destruction becomes a symbol for something subtler, but it also works in its own right. And one of the story's profoundest ironies is this: if the white men treat the blacks as animals, they become animals themselves, in a world they do not understand. The row of heads outside Kurtz's bungalow is enough to show how thin the veneer of civilization is.

The proclaimed civilizing mission of the Belgians in the Congo is clearly a recent attempt to clean up the unsavoury image of the Company. Here, Conrad directly reflects reality: the administration of the Congo – which was, for many years the private property of the Belgian monarch – became a byword even among Europeans themselves, for savage cruelty and exploitation. Whereas the French and British, however hypocritically, made genuine attempts to administer their territories in Africa honestly and humanely, the Belgians ran the Congo purely as a business proposition. Only late in the day did they attempt – unsuccessfully in Conrad's view – to acquire surface respectability for their activities; and the theme they took up was a favourite theme in Europe at the time. The idea of progress is effectively an eighteenth-century invention: behind it lies the notion that because men are infinitely capable of improving their environment through mechanical and scientific developments, there is no reason why, given time, the benefits of civilization should not be extended to the whole world. These benefits are not only material – cars, refrigerators and washing machines, better medicine and increased literacy – but moral and spiritual. If a man's environment is improved, so the argument goes, he, too, will improve: he will lose his savage habits and become a civilized human being. This view depends, of course, on a narrow definition of what constitutes civilization: something like European middle-class life at the end of the nineteenth century; and it met its first serious – indeed, devastating – challenge in the early years of our own century with the First World War (1914–1918) which revealed to a horrified Europe that savagery was not the sole domain of black, brown and yellow men, but lived at the very heart of so-called civilization itself. The unbelievable slaughter of that war, in tens of millions, inflicted a shock on Europe from which she has never recovered; but sensitive observers, even before the war, were aware of the evils of violence within their own societies. While Conrad could not possibly have anticipated the War, of course – though he lived to see it and survive it – his European stories – especially two great novels, *Under Western Eyes* (1911) and *The Secret Agent* (1907) – are filled with violence; and in *Heart of Darkness* he shows a profound understanding of the white man's civilized capacity for brutality and murder. Such an understanding suggested to him that the idea of progress was a sentimental myth, an example of wishful thinking based on the largely accidental development of a sophisticated technological culture in Europe. And in his eyes this technology not only served to mask the underlying savagery: it could even be brought into its service, as we see when the bomb explodes in *The Secret Agent*. This discovery was to be amply borne out in 1914, with the opening of the world's first technologically advanced war. The magnificent scientific developments of the nineteenth century, which had seemed to promise so much in the way of human improvement, were turned against humanity itself, with devastating results.

But if men cannot be more than superficially improved, what *is* their true identity? One of the nineteenth century's most shocking suggestions, immortalized in the work of Darwin, was that men are 'descended' from monkeys. Are we to conclude that they are no better? Conrad's implied answer to this question is to say: be glad that they are no worse. After all, what does increased sophistication bring but the ability to look into ourselves and discover horrors? Would it not be better if we were all so occupied by the daily tasks of life that we had no opportunity for destructive introspection? Isn't it the irony of progress that it gives us increasing opportunities, by providing leisure, to discover how very unpleasant we really are? These are the questions which underlie Marlow's speculations as he tries to work out the meaning of his experiences in the wilderness. One effect of this experience is to undercut conventional moral standards, for if men are not really the civilized creatures they seem to be, and if there is ultimately no meaning to existence, there can be no meaning to morality, either. Not only is European activity in Africa obnoxious on its own account, but the blanket of altruism under which the Company now proposes to conduct its business wouldn't even be valid if they put it into effect – which they won't. This the discovery Kurtz has made: he can no longer believe in his own fine sentiments even as words, because the ultimate realities of the wilderness show them up as nonsense. Take away the fragile social structures of Europe – which are little more than disguised conflicts and hatreds between nations and classes – and you have a chaos in which the only recognizable standard is power, and the only 'good' man one who can impose some sort of order through his authority. In other words, civilization and progress – the values for which genuinely benevolent and enlightened Europeans are arguing – are contradictory in themselves. They are ultimately based on force and repression. This was just the discovery which Freud (1856–1939) made at about the same time as Conrad, and it is a notion which has profoundly coloured our own century, which is perhaps why *Heart of Darkness* has proved so popular, provoking and enduring.

Structure and style

Structure

The basic structure of *Heart of Darkness* is perhaps the oldest and most familiar known to story-tellers: the quest. From ancient epics, such as the *Odyssey*, to the latest spy stories and science-fiction, this model appears in every known society with a narrative tradition, and it seems to correspond to fundamental human experience at a number of levels, from the superficial excitement of a search or a chase to the profoundest explorations of the emotional and spiritual life. Knights in search of the Grail, princes looking for enchanted princesses (an image Conrad invokes on p. 77), sailors chasing a golden fleece, mad scientists after a secret formula – all conform to this pattern. Conrad's novella simply takes Marlow up the Congo to a meeting with Kurtz, and then down again. Kurtz is his Grail, princess, fleece and formula, and the Congo is like the dark wood or the stormy sea: an obstacle the questers have to overcome in order to reach their goal. But of course, although all these stories have the basic quest motif in common, what they do with it varies widely from instance to instance, and Conrad's artistry is clearly evident in his very individual treatment.

To begin with, the quest itself – and this is relatively common – takes up the larger part of the story. Out of 94 pages in the Penguin edition, 71 are complete before Marlow actually encounters his objective: Kurtz. And even then, one might argue that the quest is not complete: on the contrary, the next stage has only just begun and remains unfinished even as Marlow tells his tale aboard the *Nellie*. This is part of the novella's irony: what seemed like the really difficult part of the adventure – the journey up the Congo – turns out to be as nothing to the problems Marlow encounters once he has met Kurtz. The difficulties and dangers of physical navigation are not to be compared with the insuperable moral enigma Marlow is faced with after his longed-for meeting. One might say that only at the end of the book does the real quest begin; the story itself is a prelude to what we are *not* told – though it is hinted at: Marlow's subsequent development. Ironically what Marlow calls the culminating experience of his life (p. 32) turns out to be the beginning, not the end. Thus the structure of the novella is turned inside-out. It is on the last page that we are ready to begin: as if to emphasize this point, the last words of the story return to its opening, and the tide is shown to be flowing out into the heart of darkness – the tide they are about to take. The darkness is still there. This isn't an ordinary adventure story, the evil hasn't been conquered, nor the obstacles overcome: they remain – permanently, it seems – to be encountered.

And this is the point at which *Heart of Darkness* differs from so many quest stories: it remains essentially incomplete and introductory, as though the real story is one we have not been told. Nor could we be told it, for the unstated narrative 'behind' what is said belongs to the realm of the inexpressible – that is its whole point: if Marlow could say what he meant, he would be able to conclude the story by making a comprehensive statement about his experience. Because he cannot, it seems that – like his prototype, Coleridge's Ancient Mariner – he is doomed for ever to repeat his story. This is the message of the ending.

Within the story which *is* told, Conrad weaves a whole range of subtle and fantastic variations on the quest pattern. Take, for example, the people Marlow encounters on his way. Traditionally, the knight or pilgrim, meets with discouragement and positive obstruction to his journey. In one famous example, Bunyan's *Pilgrim's Progress* (1678), the path to virtue and salvation is littered with bogs and giants who test the Pilgrim's resolution. Marlow, too, comes across such figures: the Manager, the Chief Brickmaker, the pilgrims; but he also meets helpers – the Patched Man, for example. The distinction between help and hindrance on his quest is also subtly blurred by Kurtz's Intended, whose very championship proves an obstacle to Marlow's deeper understanding, though in the end it helps him to understand the complexity of his experience, even as it prevents him from mastering it.

Also a part of the story as told is the complex analogy between Marlow's physical and spiritual journeys. The points at which the two do or do not match are important pointers to the novella's meaning. At the beginning his quest is a purely practical, professional one, it seems: he wants a job. However, there are enough indications to show that there is more to it than this: since childhood Marlow has been curious about the blank spaces on the map. Now, though he takes the job out of necessity –' the ships wouldn't even look at me' (p.32) – he is nevertheless also aware of stronger motives – 'The snake had charmed me' (p.33).

Marlow tells us that he always went his own way – and the phrase suggests that deliberate choice of a personal odyssey. Although he treats his preparations for the voyage out in a comic spirit – giving an almost farcical account of the accident which produced the vacancy he has filled (p. 34) – his arrival in Brussels begins to suggest the seriousness of his enterprise; and while he continues, in a thoroughly English tradition to see the comic side of things throughout most of his voyage, the situation becomes more and more serious and even tragic as the journey progresses. The relationship between comedy and tragedy points to the structural relationship between physical and spiritual adventures: the further Marlow goes, the more he becomes obsessed with the idea of Kurtz, and the more he becomes involved in a kind of oblique self-examination. Travelling to the heart of Africa he is travelling to the centre of himself – not just as an individual but as a representative of 'civilized' values; as a man created by everything European culture stands for. The journey thus becomes a multiple one: into Africa, into Marlow, into the relationship between Europe and Africa, the relationship between Europe and herself. Kurtz, the apparent objective, is really just the occasion of Marlow's obsessions. Just as the Grail is of little value in itself, so Kurtz seems to stand for the problems troubling Marlow – problems which, he hints, have troubled him long before he arrived in Africa. This experience is only the culminating point – his own term – of a long process. Thus we can also say that if the quest is not completed by his trip, it is not even initiated by it, but began long before, perhaps with the dawning of Marlow's consciousness itself, or at the moment when, as a boy, he was excited by the blank spaces on the map. The physical journey he makes up the Congo must therefore be seen in the larger perspective of Marlow's life and character – which is why Conrad so carefully prepares the story with his elaborate introduction. This introduction is an essential part of the novella's structure, not merely an excuse to tell the tale. We are returned to the story's opening at the end in order to focus our attention on this point: heart of darkness, as the last words of the text tell us, is not 'in' Africa, anymore than it is 'in' anywhere else: it is everywhere, pervasive like water, endless like the surface of the oceans on the globe. So the story, too, is circular, returning us to the start only to make us relive it, to do what Marlow has done, and go on a retrospective journey through *our* experience of *his* experience.

Style

What strikes one immediately about this text is the insistence of certain words and images – most obviously 'darkness', but also a cluster of terms associated with it, either by analogy or contrast: fog, gloom, stillness, uncertainty, gleaming, glitter, fire, shining. These words and their synonyms recur again and again, and they derive from the fundamental metaphor on which the story is based: a journey into the heart of darkness which proves in certain senses illuminating. The paradox of darkness casting light is not new to Conrad. Significantly enough, it is common in mystical literature and there is a famous example in the poetry of Henry Vaughan, who describes God as a 'deep but dazzling darkness'. Had Conrad known this poem, he might well have taken an epigraph from it, though his own darkness only casts a fitful light, and he also reverses the metaphor to show how light may in turn darken. The complex relationship between light and dark is adumbrated in the open pages of the story, which clearly show that the two are not simple opposites: they need and contain one another. On p. 28 we are told that the mist gives out light, and that the gloom in the west is actually aggravated by the approach of the sun. Then the light of day is transformed into the 'light of abiding memories' and the physical and emotional mingle. Later, the darkness appears to *produce* lights: as the sun sets, they appear upon the shore (p. 29) and London is described as:

'a brooding gloom in sunshine, a lurid glare under the stars.'

At the end of the novella this insistent mingling of light and shade is picked up in the figure of Kurtz's Intended. In the dusky room she comes towards Marlow:

'... all in black, with a pale head ... The room seemed to have grown darker, as if all the sad light of the cloudy evening had taken refuge on her forehead ...'

The girl has an 'ashy halo' and, as they talk, the darkness deepens while her fair hair seems 'to catch all the remaining light'. But the light it shines with is the sinister, the 'unearthly glow' of an illusion – the illusion of Kurtz's nobility and faithfulness. In other words, this light – described in deliberately traditional sentimental terms: the Dickensian heroine with a golden halo – is a deception. More truthful is the dark glitter of her eyes, filled with tears, anticipated before the girl enters by the 'dark gleams' of the piano, the indistinct shining of the furniture and the twilight in the luminous windows – luminous, as it were, with darkness. It is not unequivocal light which tells what truth there is, but the light and dark in twilight. Dusk is the story's permanent element, and it is dusk in which Marlow chooses that he and the girl will remain. He doesn't tell her the truth because:

'It would have been too dark, too dark altogether.'

The lie, which produces a false 'illumination' , is better – neither black nor white, but twilight.

Much of the story's force here is in the language and the memories it stirs. The luminous dusk of the three windows for example, recalls the dusky stream of the beginning. The dusk even becomes embodied at this point – seems to whisper 'The horror! The horror!' (p. 21) And this is not an isolated instance: persistently through the text men are seen as objects and objects as human: even the forest becomes a body with breath, a face and eyes. Paralleling this is the complex inter-relationship of feelings and things: just as the forest becomes a body, so it also takes on emotional qualities, it becomes more than symbolic. The landscape has a life of its own – and that life is sinister.

These aspects of language and imagery are included within the framework of the first-person narrative, which is itself complicated by several factors. To begin with, although Marlow tells the story, his story is framed by Conrad's own narration. He does not speak to us quite at first hand. Then, within Marlow's story, other people tell *their* stories, most of them concerned, directly or indirectly, with Kurtz. At times this story within a story method becomes extremely complex – as when Conrad tells us what Marlow told him about what the Patched Man told Marlow about what Kurtz told the Patched Man! This deepens the perspective of the story, giving it a greater illusion of solidity; but the principal purpose of such devices in this book is to establish Kurtz at the heart of the story – the heart of its title. Thus we come to him through a series of accounts which both reveal and conceal him, making the final effect extremely complex and increasing the uncertainty of the conclusion. A curious paradox results: while, as we have seen, the language and the imagery of the text constantly insist on a narrow range of associations – light/dark, mystery, concealment – which refer directly both to Kurtz himself and to the truth he represents for Marlow, the intricacies of the narrative blur and widen the story's points of reference so that the reader may quite literally end by not knowing what to think. And in fact, as I have suggested, if we examine the linguistic texture carefully enough, we discover that its evident simplicity – the opposition of light and dark, the quest for a mystery – is not simple at all. The paradox vanishes when we realize that the extreme care, detail and intricacy of the narrative – which we might expect to produce an effect of the greatest clarity – do the opposite. The style, in other words, is party to the whole drift of the story, which is to confront us not with an answer but with a series of questions.

General questions

1 What evidence is there to support the view that *Heart of Darkness* is really about Marlow's inner voyage of discovery?

Guideline notes for an answer

Marlow's opening disclaimer about not bothering his audience with personal experience is treated ironically – then he talks about 'the effect of it on me'. His character is carefully established at the outset – he often talks about his 'inconclusive experiences'. He refers back to his childhood ambitions. He dislikes the Belgian cynicism and is disturbed by their treatment of the natives. He talks about holding on to the facts of life, even while becoming more introspective. In Chapter 2, he becomes obsessed with Kurtz in a way which reflects on himself, and begins to think of the forest as alive and threatening. Once they begin the river journey he begins to retreat into himself – he has little contact with the others. He begins to talk about 'inborn strength' and the emotional and mental qualities a man needs to face the wilderness. He cannot distinguish between dream and reality, and is deeply upset by the helmsman's death. In the last chapter he contemplates the meaning of Kurtz's life and tries to relate it to his own.

In addition to this, the symbolism overwhelmingly suggests a journey a) inward b) into what is hidden c) into the incomprehensible; and the body imagery, centred on the idea of the heart, reinforces this.

2 There are three women playing small roles in the text. What are these roles and are they comparable?
3 Does Marlow express views about colonialism? If so, what are they?
4 Does the text give Marlow any characteristics which are perceived as typically English? Are the Belgians similarly characterized?
5 What is the purpose of Marlow's extended introduction to his story?
6 Why is the novella called *Heart of Darkness*?

7 How often does the word 'darkness' (or dark) occur in the story, and what effect does it have?

8 In what ways does Conrad use the quest motif?

9 What is the purpose of making the story's ending echo its beginning?

10 What does Marlow learn from his experience?

11 What are we expected to make of Kurtz? Is a clear view expressed in the book, and if so, is it Marlow's or Conrad's?

12 What does ivory symbolize in this book?

13 How are Europe and Africa compared or contrasted?

14 Give a careful analysis of the story's time-scale and the role this plays in *Heart of Darkness*.

15 What part does comedy play in this novella?

16 To what extent might one legitimately call *Heart of Darkness* an adventure story?

Further reading

The best critical biography of Conrad is:

Joseph Conrad: The Three Lives, by Frederick Karl (New York 1979)
Conrad's Western World, by Norman Sherry (CUP 1971) is also excellent
on the background to the novelist's work and his sources.